Be SMARTER than a
CEO
IN 30 DAYS

J.J. Medney

This page intentionally left blank.

Be SMARTER than a CEO IN 30 DAYS

J. J. Medney

LEGAL AND COPYRIGHT NOTICE

This book is written as a source of information only. The book is sold with the understanding that the author and publisher are not engaged in the rendering of legal, accounting or other professional services. If professional assistance is required, then the services of an appropriate professional should be engaged.

The author and publisher make no representations or warranties with respect to the accuracy or completeness of the contents of the work. The advice and strategies contained herein may not be suitable for every situation. The author and the publisher expressly disclaim responsibility for any adverse effects arising from the use or application of the information contained herein.

The fact that a book or organization or website is referred to in this work as a citation and/or a potential source of further information does not mean that the author or publisher endorses such information. Readers should also be aware that listed websites may have changed or have been discontinued between the time this book was written and when it is read.

TABLE OF CONTENTS

This page intentionally left blank.

INTRODUCTION

LET'S GET ACQUAINTED

Received both a Bachelor's and Master's Degree in finance from Columbia University and a Bachelor of Laws from St. John's University. Later, admitted as an attorney in the State of New York. As for military service, flew with the 94th Bomber Group and was awarded the Distinguished Flying Cross.

Have represented listed companies ranging from General Electric to ITT (when it controlled Avis, Sheraton and Hartford Insurance) to American Realty & Petroleum. By the same token, I have handled numerous small and medium enterprises (SMEs) and am well aware of their burden in securing product, obtaining financing, recruiting staff, generating customers and operating a business with limited funds.

Have built, owned and managed multiple operations in 10 states with corporate offices in New York City and Atlanta.

Have given numerous Seminar Presentations nationally ranging from N.Y. Professional Groups to the Atlanta Chamber of Commerce to Las Vegas visitors.

Have written numerous articles appearing in such diverse publications as the N.Y. Times and the N.Y. Law Journal.

WHY DO TALENTED BUSINESS PEOPLE FAIL?

In today's complex marketplace, you need more than just a specialized skill to be successful. Simply knowing accounting or marketing or selling or technology or production is not enough. To move ahead requires something more. And that something more is—an awareness and understanding of what makes a company grow and become profitable.

This is why in writing *Be Smarter Than a CEO in 30 Days*, I brought together the insight and wisdom of over 50 business leaders—luminaries ranging from Mark Zuckerberg (Facebook), Sam Palmisano (IBM), and Larry Page (Google) to former CEOs as Jack Welch (GE), Louis Gerstner (IBM) and Lewis Platt (HP).

I then packaged their know-how into every phase of operating a profitable business. You will gain a broad-based understanding of strategy, customers, marketing, innovation, management, product lines, knowledge employees, entrepreneurship, going global, business ethics—even how to interpret a financial statement.

A world of knowledge will be passed on to you.

THE ESSENCE OF CREATIVITY

Isaac Newton, the eminent physicist, observed that if he could see farther than most, it was because he stood on the shoulders of giants. He meant, of course, a wealth of information came before him from the likes of Copernicus and Galileo. Besides being a gracious acknowledgment of those who preceded him,

Newton's comment also reflected on the "essence of creativity." It is built on a foundation.

None of Newton's predecessors taught him calculus or the laws of motion or the theory of tides, comets and gravity. Yet he openly admitted that it was "their teachings" that paved the way for his unparalleled productivity.

This concept of learning from the wisdom of others—as the starting point for one's own knowledge base—is one of the underlying principles of the book.

THE CHALLENGE OF CHANGE

As business people today, we are facing an unprecedented "challenge of change." The forces driving this change can be attributed to 1) the explosive growth in technology 2) an ever-shifting and globalized marketplace and 3) the emergence of knowledge workers—people who bring their own tools to the job site every day—their brainpower.

In meeting this challenge, American business literature has had its shortcomings. Many of the strategy and how-to books have been too narrowly focused. The success story of one firm or even a group of companies may not be applicable to you or your organization. Then again, the works of many professors often have been too ethereal and lacked front-line experience.

All this is not meant to be critical, it is just that change is taking place so rapidly that yesterday's success formula will not cut it in today's marketplace. Lewis Platt, former CEO of Hewlett-Packard, said it best, "The single biggest problem in business is staying with your previously successful business model…one year too long."

Therefore, rather than concentrating on company success stories which may not be relevant—why not focus on the "empowerment of you?" I guarantee that once you have absorbed the fundamentals and guidelines presented in the forthcoming chapters, you will have the know-how to tackle virtually any company concern you are likely to encounter.

PROFIT OR PERISH

While some high-priced consultants may have a cavalier attitude toward profitability as just "bean counting"—do not buy into it. The duality of generating cash flow and profitability are the life-sustaining organs of the organization. Keep losing money and you will not stay in business very long.

This is why every chapter in *Be Smarter Than a CEO in 30 Days* contains guidelines that will transport you from concept to income-producing commerce.

Clayton Christensen, in his ground-breaking book, *The Innovator's Dilemma*, noted that even the best-run companies can become candidates for failure due to "disruptive technology." Discounters, operating on low profit margins and offering aggressively priced products can siphon off many of the larger company's most loyal customers.

Yes, not every event in business is controllable and worst-case scenarios do happen. Nevertheless, there are actions of awareness and adaptability that can meet the challenge head-on. The key is for an astute CEO to structure all phases of the operation so that they work together to produce the highest probability for profitability.

This is our target, and this is what you will encounter all along the way.

THE "KISS" PRINCIPLE: KEEP IT SIMPLE AND SHORT

One of my highest priorities is taking every major component of operating a business—and bring it down to size. In other words, keep it simple. However, do not confuse simplicity with superficiality.

I am reminded of Jack Welch's response to two questions raised by the famed management guru Peter Drucker, "Simple questions, but like much that is simple, they are also profound."

Thus, throughout the treatise I will follow the KISS principle. My goal is to turn complexity into simplicity. The reward shall be knowledge that not only makes sense, but is actionable in the daily course of commerce.

YOUR PERSONAL KNOWLEDGE MACHINE

Let's talk about you. Whether you are a guy or gal climbing the corporate ladder or an entrepreneur managing a small or mid-sized firm—your personal success will depend upon your contribution to the enterprise's earnings.

This is where *Be Smarter Than a CEO in 30 Days* can play a major role.

You will gain access to every essential phase in generating a company's top-line growth and bottom-line profit. Each chapter will present step-by-step checklists and guidelines. Think of it as having your own personal coach each step of the way.

You will soon be able to converse with anyone—on any level, on any topic—and feel very comfortable. If the conversation gravitates to strategy, you will be armed with a 10-point strategic plan for companies large and small. If the subject turns to advertising, you will have at your command the nine basic issues covering *Market *Message*Media. People will marvel at your newfound knowledge.

You will be offered a series of sophisticated business tactics that I have employed over the years. You will learn the "napkin strategy." How—on the dry side of a cocktail napkin—you can analyze a company in just seven numbers. Yes, it works even better after the second martini!

You will encounter my "shoestring strategy"—a low-cost marketing strategy for sizing up what the customer wants, needs and is willing to pay for. This minimal-cost initiative can produce high-value customer data.

The book goes on like this page after page. Your knowledge of business will grow and expand beyond anything you could have imagined. A flow of opportunities will surely unfold.

Let us begin our journey together.

CHAPTER 1
STRATEGY

STRATEGY DEFINED

Strategy is one of the most powerful and commanding terms in the language of business. It instantly draws attention because it embraces a "plan of action."

In a nutshell, strategy is all about having a realistic plan to attain specific objectives.

Let us now take a panoramic view of strategy through the eyes of six renowned strategists by highlighting excerpts from their writings.

STRATEGIC POSITIONING

There are many highly regarded strategists, but only one Michael E. Porter. For our purposes, we begin with his article in the *Harvard Business Review* titled "What Is Strategy?"

Porter begins by distinguishing between "operational effectiveness" and strategy. "Operational effectiveness" relates to the company's ability to outperform competition and post higher profits. The problem with this competitive advantage, however, is that it is short-lived. Competitors can soon duplicate the process and with newer technology even exceed the company's best efforts.

Porter's response is to use "strategic positioning." He calls upon the company to focus on what makes it distinctive and different. He cites Southwest Airline, a company that focuses on providing low-cost, convenient services to selected destinations. Compare this strategic positioning to full-service airlines that are committed to all the intricacies of pricing and routing passengers domestically and globally.

Thus, Porter's response to "What is strategy?" can be summed up as follows, "Strategy is the creation of a unique and valuable position...and the essence of strategic positioning is to choose activities that are different from rivals."

COMPETING FOR THE FUTURE

Gary Hamel and C.K. Prahalad are two outstanding academic consultants from the University of Michigan who authored *Competing for the Future.*

They begin with, "Our starting premise is simple: competition for the future is competition to create and dominate emerging opportunities." This means transforming the company to adopt a strategic agenda to1) reshape its product line 2) redesign corporate processes and 3) redirect its resources.

Another critically important concept advanced in the book centers around the need to concentrate on the company's "core competencies." The authors call upon organizations to focus on what they do best rather than on what they are currently doing. This is an essential strategy in dominating future emerging opportunities.

Honda is a classic example of a company that has leveraged its core competencies. In addition to a line of highly rated automobiles, it also produces outboard motors, lawnmowers, off-road vehicles and indoor generators.

3

ALL THE RIGHT MOVES

Professor Constantinos C. Markides of the London Business School wrote a refreshingly clear approach to designing a winning strategy in, *All the Right Moves: A Guide to Crafting Breakthrough Strategy.*

He relates strategic positioning to how a company responds to three basic questions.

- Who should we target as customers?

- What products or services should we offer?

- How can we best deliver them?

The professor proclaims that the goal for every company should be to answer these questions differently from its competitors, thereby formulating its own strategic position. Management must then build an organization with the corporate culture to support and implement the right strategic choices. Strategic positioning alone will not get it done.

STRATEGY FOR BIG BLUE

Who Says Elephants Can't Dance? by Louis V. Gerstner provides a unique insight into the strategy he employed in the IBM turnaround.

He questioned whether IBM should remain committed to producing competitive hardware that was fast becoming a commoditized product with low profit margins. Why not, he reasoned, have IBM—with its superb research and

4

development, global presence and vast capabilities—become a service and solution company?

Certainly, the market existed. The worldwide business community was drowning in underperforming high technology. In addition, it was suffering from a hodgepodge of software and hardware components that were either incompatible or ineffective.

Of course, revitalizing customer focus, reducing mountainous overhead and turning around an entrenched corporate culture are further testaments to his innovative strategies and managerial insight.

The acquisition of PricewaterhouseCoopers, the sale of the computer division to the Chinese firm, Lenovo, and the follow-up management practices of his successor, Sam Palmisano—are lasting tributes to Gerstner's strategic legacy.

THE STRATEGY PARADOX

In *The Strategy Paradox*, author Michael E. Raynor employs an age-old technique in writing and lecturing. He sets up the dragon and then proceeds to slay it.

The dragon in *Paradox* stems from the fact that commitments made today may differ considerably from projected future events—and this accounts for "strategic uncertainty." Raynor offers a four-part approach to managing this uncertainty as follows 1) work up additional future scenarios 2) prepare a full-blown strategy for each scenario 3) determine when to use one of these options and 4) manage this collection of options.

The author is a highly regarded strategist with Deloitte Consulting. His solutions are brilliantly conceived, however they apply to very large companies with vastly longer time horizons. For the majority of firms operating on a yearly timeframe, there is a simpler solution to "strategic uncertainty" which will be covered in the forthcoming chapter "The Art of Management."

STRAIGHT FROM THE GUT

In *Jack: Straight from the Gut by* Jack Welch, there are enough strategies to fill our entire treatise. Let's highlight just two:

The great American management guru Peter Drucker contributed to the first. Drucker questioned, "If you weren't already in the business, would you enter it today?" And if the answer is no, "What are you going to do about it?"

Welch's reaction was, "Simple questions—but like much that is simple, they were also profound." This led Welch to a strategy of insisting that every GE company had to be No. 1 or No. 2 in every business they were in. The sub-strategy then became "fix, sell or close."

Another strategy that Welch championed was the Motorola practice of Six Sigma. Technically, it relates to reducing defective parts to only 3.4 per million. Welch turned this quality-control concept into a leadership mind-set that focused on improving all facets of the business and reaching out to customers.

Six Sigma wasn't just a GE mantra. The company's compensation plan was changed so that 60 percent of bonuses were financially based, while 40 percent were tied to Six Sigma performance.

A STRATEGIC PLAN FOR YOUR COMPANY

Here, in a summary format, is a 10-point strategic plan that can serve the needs of companies both large and small.

1) Strategy begins with a "vision" of where the company is headed. A pilot does not take off without filing a flight plan and plotting a destination. It is imperative to have the company's "vision" effectively communicated to the entire organization.

2) Establish short-term benchmarks against which strategic performance can be measured. Marketing should forecast realistic top-line growth. Production should be coordinated and quality controlled. Accounting must stand behind its cost estimates and profitability projections.

3) Strategy should focus on the duality of improving current operations while seeking to launch new projects. Lewis Platt, former head of Hewlett-Packard, understood this need for a company to reinvent itself. He offered, "We have to be willing to cannibalize what we are doing today in order to ensure our leadership in the future."

4) The entire organization should participate in strategic planning. Management must place its faith

in its knowledge employees and realize they are its most valuable long-term asset. It also must recognize and reward outstanding performances.

5) Management must direct all strategies toward satisfying customer needs in real time. It must establish a customer-centered culture and create a customer-oriented product line.

6) Market research should underlie all marketing campaigns. Advertising should be based on the three M's of *Market*Message*Media. All campaigns should be test marketed prior to a full-scale launch.

7) Developing a company's "core competencies" is essential strategy for improving operation and generating new products. It enables a company to expand its products and services to better serve customer needs in a changing environment.

8) Managing a company's "operating strategy" is a four-step process. It begins with the company projecting operations for the forthcoming year, on a monthly basis. Then, each month's actual results are compared to the projection. The variances are accounted for and any required changes are immediately acted upon.

9) Strategizing solely on data accumulated inside the organization is an invitation to disaster. The company must look beyond the corporate four walls. Relevant information should be gathered on customers, prospects, competitors, emerging technologies, global markets and all other impact

factors. Armed with internal data and outside information, management then can effectively conceive and execute innovative strategies.

10) For many companies, 95% of their prospective customers live outside the USA. This means that going global offers a strategy to open new markets, increase profits, locate less costly components and respond to foreign requests for proposals.

Let me suggest you take particular note of this 10-point strategic guideline. It is highly significant and I will be developing more of its content as we move forward. Be mindful that these strategies are not just for larger companies.

STRATEGY IS FOR ALL COMPANIES

I am reminded of a law firm that faced a strategy crisis that had nothing to do with law.

The firm had built a fine practice of representing major Florida developers in preparing legal documents for registering in New York State. Upon acceptance, the Florida developers could then advertise and sell their residential properties in the huge New York market.

Since the law firm had a New York office with local attorneys, it decided to go after the larger New York developers. The firm soon discovered that these big-time real estate developers were totally captured by the large New York law firms. There was no way to penetrate.

This was not a legal problem. Rather, the dilemma can be framed as, "What strategy does a company employ when its competitors gain control of the marketplace?"

I was called upon to find a solution.

- First, I did some market research and soon realized they had the wrong "vision." In metro New York City, there are some 20,000 smaller apartment buildings that also could use the law firm's services. I then devised a two-phase strategy.

- The initial phase was to gain local recognition. I then had the law firm hire a top public relations agency specializing in the real estate field. Within six months, articles about the firm appeared in the *New York Times*, *New York Law Journal*, *Real Estate Weekly*, local newspapers and numerous trade publications. I then had the agency prepare a four-page montage of these prestigious articles.

- It was now time for the second phase—getting business. A series of direct-mail campaigns were launched to the 20,000 building owners containing a one-page letter, the four-page montage (for credibility) and an invitation to attend an "educational seminar." In addition to the law firm, guest speakers included members of major accounting firms and real estate brokerages. In a single session, building owners discovered the entire legal process of condominium and co-op conversions.

- Six months later, the New York volume exceeded the Florida billings.

There is much to be learned from this brief example—from seeking out a "niche" market to employing direct response marketing.

All of this and more will be covered in later chapters. For now, I want you to recognize that strategy is critical for enterprises of all sizes and in all endeavors.

A PERSONAL STRATEGY

So far, we have covered strategy from a company viewpoint. How about a strategy for you? Well, here is one I have employed successfully for many years.

I cannot attend a conference or exit a meeting or even read a document without evaluating it by asking myself, "Was it better or different—or neither"?

To fully grasp this approach, let us distinguish between better and different.

BETTER

Many senior managers are preoccupied with "doing things better" in order to meet Wall Street's quarterly projections. They focus on improving all phases of the company's operation, ranging from gaining market share to reducing personnel to lowering costs.

Just strategizing to "do things better," however, is a prescription for competitive penetration. Product excellence can be copied and exceeded by newer technology. By reducing prices and improving customer services, competitors can capture all but the most loyal customers.

Therefore, the near-term advantage of doing things "better" can soon vanish on the competitive battleground. Something more is required for long-term success.

DIFFERENT

That "something more" is the innovative strategy of doing things that are "different" from the competition.

The success stories of organizations that have done things differently are legendary. They include Dell's selling computers direct-to-customers via the internet, Southwest Airlines and its no-frills flying, Swatch and it switch to low- price Swiss timepieces, British Airway's enriched customer services, Wal-Mart's launching discount retailing in less populated communities and on and on.

Of course, the combination of being both better and different cannot be matched by the competition.

Therefore, develop the mind-set of evaluating everything you hear, see or read in terms of "Was it better or different—or neither?" The strategy will serve you well, as it has for me.

THE WRAP-UP

Let's look at what we have gathered from our discussion on strategy.

- Strategy is all about having a realistic plan to attain specific objectives.
- "Operational effectiveness" is a short-term advantage that competitors can overtake.
- Strategic positioning is crucially important and involves choosing those activities that are different from competitors.
- To be primed for future opportunities, a company should adopt a strategy that revitalizes all its resources— people, products and processes.
- Focusing on "core competencies" (what the company does best) is an essential strategy for satisfying customer needs and creating new products.
- Another approach to strategic positioning lies in how a company responds differently from its competitors in customer selection, products offered and services delivered.
- Switching from a commoditized (similar to competitors) product line with low profit margins to products and services with higher margins is a top innovative strategy.
- As demonstrated at IBM, company-wide strategy needs to go beyond people and product lines and must incorporate greater customer focus, cost containment and a change in corporate culture.

- A strategy paradox arises from commitments made today that may differ considerably— from projected future events. The proposed solution lies in working up a collection of future scenarios with accompanying strategies to be employed as future events dictate.
- Jack Welch's strategy of having every GE company be No.1 or No. 2 in its industry can be imitated by a small firm having a single product—and making certain that it rates first or second in the field.
- At General Electric, Six Sigma became a data-driven systematic approach to problem solving with particular emphasis on impacting the customer.
- Strategy for companies large and small should embrace,

> 1) establishing a "vision"
> 2) setting performance benchmarks
> 3) "cannibalizing what we are doing today to ensure leadership in the future"
> 4) co-workers participating in strategic planning
> 5) establishing a customer-centered culture and customer-oriented product line
> 6) focusing marketing campaigns on research and the three M's of *Market *Message*Media
> 7) developing a company's "core competencies"
> 8) projecting operations on a monthly basis— then comparing actual results to the projection, accounting for variances and acting upon any required changes

9) recognizing that strategy based solely on internal data is an invitation to disaster and
10) going global and opening new markets

- Strategic planning is not the exclusive domain of the larger companies—smaller firms can drink from this well, as well.
- The success stories of companies that have done things "differently" are legendary. Think Dell, Southwest Airlines, Swatch, British Airways and Wal-Mart.
- Adopt a personal mind-set of viewing all activities by way of "Was it better or different—or neither."

It is now time to enter the world where the customer rules.

This page intentionally left blank.

CHAPTER 2

THE CUSTOMER RULES

CUSTOMERS AND PROFITS

The customer rules simply because the customer is the source of cash flow, profitability and everyone's next paycheck.

There is an old adage that says 20% of a company's customers produce 80% of its profits. Now, two Harvard professors, Robin Cooper and Robert S. Kaplan, have revealed the provocative 20–225% rule in their book *The Design of Cost Management Systems.* Their research showed that in some companies, 20% of a company's customers accounted for
225% of the earned profits. This naturally leads to the conclusion that 80% of customers were quite costly to the organization.

Thus, management's overriding responsibility is to increase the number of highly profitable 20% customers and replace the 80% losers.

This is also a good time to eradicate the 1990s mind-set of "let's build market share and everything else will fall into place." That is a guaranteed prescription for failure. Of course, we want to grow and increase the number of customers—but only if they are money makers.

Once we determine who the profitable 20% are, we must act boldly and institute a programmed dismissal of the losing customers. Fewer losers equals more profits.

SATISFACTION AND SOLUTIONS

What if we ask the CEO of a product-centric organization, "How should a company go about satisfying the needs of its customers?"

Chances are, the CEO would offer a laundry list of benefits such as lower prices, higher quality, new design features, faster delivery, making it longer lasting, creating ease in purchasing, greater choices and superior services before and after the sale.

If we pose the same question to the CEO of a consumer-centric enterprise, however, the first response would be "providing customer solutions." Today, customers are more attracted to products that provide solutions than to the ones with all the bells and whistles.

Adrian Slywotzky and David Morrison, in their acclaimed book *The Profit Zone*, said it best, "The key driver will be customer relevance (what they need, want, willing to pay for), rather than a focus on what a company knows what to do. If a skill is relevant to a customer and is not currently offered, the company must develop it, or hire it, or acquire it, or license it, or find a business partner who will provide it."

It is critical to recognize that providing solutions and satisfaction leads to one of the company's most valuable assets—loyal customers. Recent reports have shown that, depending on the industry, it costs five to eight times more to get a new customer than retain an existing one.

Chris Denove and James D. Power IV, of J. D. Power and Associates, have produced a classic book titled *Satisfaction: How Every Great Company Listens to the Voice of the*

Customer. Through the findings of responsive surveys, they document how increased customer satisfaction correlates to bottom-line results and increased stockholder value.

They set forth the basic requirements.

1. Management's fostering a culture of satisfying the customer

2. Rewarding customer-focused personnel

3. Building a customer-centric infrastructure based on the survey responses

SATISFYING THE CUSTOMER IN "REAL TIME"

Regis McKenna, the high-tech marketing whiz and SiliconValley guru, offers a fresh insight into customer relationship. In Real Time: Preparing for the Age of the Never Satisfied Customer, he calls for focusing on the short-term needs of the customer, rather than long-range strategic planning. This, he claims, will be the best guarantor of long-term success. He argues that one does not prepare for a marathon by running marathons but by daily shorter sprints.

To meet the growing demand for customized services, he proposes that organizations install dynamic information systems that can respond in "real time." Such innovative technology enables company personnel to connect and respond promptly to individual customer needs.

Jerry Yang, founder of Yahoo, sums up Regis McKenna's work this way, "The notion of eliminating hierarchy and long-term planning and creating real-time management that focuses on delivery, results and customer needs is a key revelation for companies large and small."

MANAGEMENT'S DILEMMA

As customers are offered more choices and become more demanding—market-savvy management faces a major dilemma. No organization, regardless of size or talent, can overshadow the competition in every area and remain profitable.

Instead of being all things to all customers, international consultants Jeremy and Tony Hope suggest in *Competing in the Third Wave,* "Third-wave managers are able to think like their customers. They decide which market niche to attack, build a platform of competencies to undertake the assault, and, with the backing of imaginative information systems, ensure they can deliver more value than the competition."

However, a challenging problem can arise as the niche product becomes highly successful. Soon, competitors enter the marketplace and the niche product becomes commoditized. Here, I am referring to the influx of competitive products that look alike, perform alike and are sold at lower prices. Profits and shareholder value can soon decline.

Astute and responsive management often turns to extraordinary services as a difference maker.

"FANATICAL" SERVICES

Jennifer Nastu, a principal at the PJ Writing Group (jen@mediabuyerplanner.com), recently authored an article, "How a Web Service Firm Used 'Fanatical' Customer Care to Increase Sales 60 Percent, Year over Year." It appeared as a case study in an online marketing service known as MarketingProfs (www.marketingprofs.com).

The case study tells the story of Rackspace, a Texas webhosting firm, whose management made an all-out commitment to provide "fanatical" customer service. It trademarked the term "Fanatical Support," placed it on employee T-shirts, highlighted it on its web site and featured the theme throughout all marketing campaigns.

It enabled a small company to outpace the competition in the crowded and commoditized field of web hosting.

EXTREME CUSTOMER SERVICE

In a recent issue of *Fortune Small Business* magazine, the cover story headline was "Extreme Customer Service." It starts out with noting that "Surveys show that more consumers than ever are fed up with bad service." It then goes on to reveal how some small firms are stealing customers away from large, impersonal stores.

I found the Kassie Rempel story particularly intriguing. Kassie founded a company named Simply Soles. It's an online women's shoe emporium specializing in high-fashion, high-cost designer shoes. Kassie sends out a selection of shoes to established customers and only bills them for shoes purchased. The others are returned in prepaid mailers at a $12 charge per pair.

For the female executive, it is like having a boutique shoe store around the corner.

I guess my attraction to Kassie's operation was twofold. First, strategy-wise, it met the test of being both better and different. Next, customer-wise, she solved her customer's needs and satisfied them with unmatched services.

WHEN THINGS GO WRONG

Chances are, somewhere down the road, there is going to be a major mess-up with one of your customers—or a whole bunch of them. Think JetBlue and its flight cancellations or Menu Foods and adulterated cat and dog food.

Jeanne Bliss (www.customerbliss.com) recently wrote an article for MarketingProfs titled "Seven Actions to Regain Customer Trust When Things Go Wrong." The article centers on communicating frequently, actively and passionately.

Bliss advocates taking immediate action and issuing a heartfelt apology. Next, make the customer as "whole" as possible, as soon as possible. Follow Jeanne Bliss, and you could save loyal customers, as well as make new ones along the way.

GLOBAL OR LOCAL—THE STORY IS THE SAME

Jay R. Galbraith is a highly regarded international authority on organizational design. Based on three years of research at the McKinsey Organization, he produced a notable work, *Designing the Customer-Centric Organization.*

His opening theme projects the downward spiral of product-centric organizations because, sooner or later, products tend to become commoditized.

His solution, of course, is the customer-centric organization. However, the tough part is in the transition. Major changes must take place in orienting the entire organization to focus on generating and maintaining loyal customers.

Interestingly, it should be noted that the underlying story is the same whether the company is a global giant or local enterprise. Customer-centricity simply implies offering products and services that provide greater value than the competition. The target is always the same—loyal and profitable customers.

CRM SOFTWARE

We have now reached the point where we need to ask, "What tools or programs can management employ in achieving greater customer satisfaction and loyalty?" A good place to start is with Customer Relationship Management (CRM) software.

For those who are not familiar, CRM software is designed to capture all phases of the interaction between the company and the customer. It covers transactions such as sales records, e-mails, phone contacts, leads, marketing campaigns and customer buying habits—all areas of communication and relationship.

Over the years, internet-based CRM has improved dramatically. Company personnel can now access the information from anywhere with any web browser. With this capability to collect and deploy information rapidly, the enterprise has an unmatched tool in responding to customer needs in "real time."

A fully integrated CRM program also can serve as a data source for departments beyond marketing and sales. For small to mid-sized firms, there are off-the-shelf CRM software packages that can be reprogrammed to meet specific company needs.

For those who want to delve farther into the world of CRM, there is Jill Dyche's *The CRM Handbook: A Business Guide to Customer Relationship Management*. Jill has done an impressive job of blending CRM fundamentals with client case studies. She covers the entire CRM landscape from product selection, to lists and quizzes to checklists of do's and don'ts. Of course, you should supplement your research with updated vendor literature.

SURVEYS

Surveys reveal *why* things happen. Survey feedback can be management's "secret weapon" in soliciting data covering:

- What customers want, need and are willing to pay for?

- Whether their products and services meet customer expectations?

- What is the customer's comfort level in dealing with company personnel?

- Which changes or improvements are recommended?

- How company products and services compare to the competition?

- Which of the company's products or services is most highly valued?

- Which product or service has failed to perform?

- Whether customer expectations mesh with reality?

- Whether the company meets or exceeds benchmarks of comparable organizations?

Interestingly, in his book *The Ultimate Question*, Fred Reichheld promotes the concept that a single question can be a predictor of success or failure. The query he suggests is, "Are you likely to recommend us to friends and colleagues?"

The key driver in all this probing is to uncover actionable feedback for management in devising strategy to retain loyal customers—and find new ones.

I personally am a firm believer in the survey process. I still cling to the old adage that a happy customer will recommend three others while an unhappy one will spread negativity to nine.

A full-service firm should have the capability to design and deploy the survey, collect the data, analyze the results, produce the report and present the findings. One firm I found with this capacity is National Business Research Institute, Inc. (www.nbrii.com), an organization of business research psychologists with over 6,000 clients and a staff of 300.

UNSTRUCTURED DATA

In general, companies formulate customer policy from the feedback of "structured data" obtained from CRM systems, surveys and various internal sources.

However, there is a wealth of vital data from unstructured sources that is overlooked because it is difficult to access and costly to assess. This information can flow from call-center notes, written responses in surveys, commentaries in e-mail exchanges, internet-generated discourse, blogs and similar communications.

Now, one firm, Clarabridge, Inc. (www.clarabridge.com), has developed sophisticated software that can transform unstructured data into actionable information. It can harvest any content via a series of "source connectors" that can tie into call centers, e-mail systems, internet sites and the like.

Once the information is sourced, Clarabridge has the technology to transform such diverse text into structured, analyzable data. This means that management can leverage the entire universe of structured and unstructured data to drive customer solutions and satisfaction.

SHOESTRING STRATEGY

I would be remiss if I concluded this chapter without revealing one of my favorite shoestring (low-cost) strategies.

There is a simple approach to unlocking what is on your customer's mind. Just book separate luncheons with your top three customers—after you have complemented them on how much you admire their insight and wisdom.

At lunch, take out a sheet of paper with the appropriate questions and simply say, "I value your thoughts too much to leave to memory, so let me jot down some notes as you speak."

At a minimum, there are three areas you must cover in obtaining hard data.

1. What does the customer realistically want, need and is willing to pay for?

2. How does the customer rate your product and what changes are recommended?

3. What is happening in the marketplace in terms of competitive products and pricing?

Lunch may be a low-cost initiative, but it can produce high-value, actionable customer data.

One final thought. Some time ago, I dealt with a medical/health company that marketed a device for improving circulation.

The organization developed a nationwide network of distributors in addition to company-owned outlets. At a national meeting, after all the motivational speakers had concluded, I held an open session with the distributors. Their product-improving suggestions were mind-blowing. The moral of this story is twofold:

1. It is not how great a product management thinks it produces, but rather how the customer reacts that is all important.

2. Your best market research may reside inside the company—the associates who interact daily with the customer.

Don't ever bypass this fountain of knowledge.

THE WRAP-UP

Now, let's see how much we have discovered about the almighty customer.

- The customer rules because the customer is the source of cash flow, profitability and everyone's next paycheck.

- It is critical to determine which customers are profitable and to unload the losers.

- We want all the customers we can get—but they must be profitable.

- Customers are more attracted to products that provide solutions than the ones with all the bells and whistles.

- "If a skill is relevant to a customer, the company must develop it, or hire it, or acquire it, or license it or find a business partner who will provide it."

- A loyal customer is one of the company's most valuable assets. It costs five to eight times more to get a new customer than retain an existing one.

- Focus on satisfying the customer in "real time" rather than long-range strategic planning.

- No company can overshadow the competition in every area and remain profitable.

- It is challenging to be profitable when marketing commoditized (similar) products. Extraordinary services can make the difference.

- Surveys show that more consumers than ever are fed up with bad service. Kassie Rempel's online shoe emporium meets the test of being both better and different as well as solving customer needs with unmatched services.

- When things go wrong, apologize and do whatever it takes— as soon as it takes—to compensate for any loss or inconvenience.

- Whether global giant or local enterprise, the focus must be on generating profitable and loyal customers.

- Savvy management should utilize CRMs vast database to formulate customer policy.

- Deploying CRM data online enables company personnel to access the information from anywhere with any web browser.

- Surveys enable management to solicit data on the entire company/customer relationship.

- The single question that can be a predictor of success or failure is, "Are you likely to recommend us to friends and colleagues?"

- A happy customer will recommend to three others while an unhappy one will spread negativity to nine.

- Unstructured data, from call-center notes to e-mail commentaries, can be accessed and converted to actionable information.

- Luncheon with top customers may be a low-cost initiative, but it can produce high-value returns.

Now, it is time to determine how to get these profitable and loyal customers. That happens to be the subject of the next chapter—Marketing.

This page intentionally left blank.

CHAPTER 3
MARKETING

"I KNOW IT WHEN I SEE IT"

As America's most revered management pundit, Peter Drucker, stated over fifty years ago in *The Practice of Management,* "Any business enterprise has two—and only these two—basic functions: innovation and marketing." From my view, it is as true today as it ever was.

Throughout our discourse, the term "marketing" shall include advertising, sales, promotions, public relations, market research, target audiences, product lines, price, distribution channels, services, competitive analysis and return on investment (ROI).

Marketing is truly the lifeblood of the organization and no company can reach its full growth potential without a market-focused management. Kevin Clancy and Peter Krieg go a step further by declaring in *Counter-Intuitive Marketing*, "We believe most strategic planning issues are fundamentally marketing decisions."

Without effective marketing, there are fewer sales, less customers and lower profits. Again, we are reminded of our basic doctrine of "Profit or Perish."

Today's CEO need not be a connoisseur of marketing, but he or she should have a cultivated appreciation of what constitutes good vs. bad marketing. The CEO should be able to exclaim, as Supreme Court Justice Potter Stewart once did when judging a case, "I know it when I see it."

My objective in this chapter is to arm you with the substance and spirit of marketing, so you too will know it when you see it.

"P" SOUP

Marketing started out like alphabet soup and then turned into "P" soup. It began with the four P's, standing for product, price, place and promotion. Then, as we began marketing "services", we encountered the seven P's when people, process and physical evidence were added. To accommodate the internet aficionados, four more P's came along— personalization, participation, peer-to-peer and predictive modeling. Now, the customer-centric crowd wants us to buy into the five P's of people, passion, processes, platform and partners.

Wow— Positively prohibitive!

THE THREE M's

In line with my commitment to the KISS principle of "keeping it simple and short"— let us recognize that marketing soup can also be condensed into the three M's of *Market*Message*Media. Literally, the who, what and where of marketing.

- Who is the target <u>Market</u>?

- What <u>Message</u> will motivate them to buy the product or service?

- Where is the best <u>Media</u> for reaching the target market? Is it newspapers, magazines, TV, internet, radio, cell phones or direct mail?

While the three M's formula bypasses much of what is in "P" soup, it very nicely meets my prime objective. Instead of being caught in the multiple tentacles of marketing, I can best serve you by concentrating on how a company "moves merchandise." This is accomplished by generating customers—and that is what the three M's are all about.

"WHAT IF"

Einstein had his "thought experiments" from whence flowed his theory of relativity and its implication for movement, space and time. I wish we were all that smart.

However, we can find immense value from thought-provoking questions that arise from the "What if" scenario. Let's try it out on the three M's.

"What if" you are asked to head-up a company that has a new product—that is priced right, performs as claimed and the entire organization is excited about its potential. In fact, the company recently hired a top-notch local advertising agency to prepare a campaign.

The agency has just called and is ready to make their presentation. Although this is your first day at the company and you are unfamiliar with the new product—what three basic questions would you want the ad agency to answer in each of the three M's? Here is how you might prepare for the conference.

Market

1. Has the company or agency performed any market research to determine whether the product is right for this targeted market?

2. Are there niche sectors within the overall market where the company can dominate and avoid competition?

3. Before the company commits the advertising budget, can the campaign be test marketed to determine what works best and what should be avoided?

Message

1. Does the message reflect the product's ability to solve and satisfy customer problems?

2. Does the message address the product's benefits in terms of performance, price, design, color selection, ease of usage, availability and services after sale?

3. Have alternate headlines and body copy been prepared for test marketing the campaign and have various incentives been considered?

Media

1. Will the proposed media reach the largest target audience at the lowest cost per prospect?

2. Can a lower-cost internet strategy such as pay-per-click or e-mail be employed to test market the campaign?

3. In addition to testing headlines and body copy, has the agency considered testing competitive media such as e-mail vs. direct mail?

The ad agency should be positioned to respond to all questions. If market research has not taken place, then ask, "How could your firm prepare a marketing campaign without this information?"

A well-thought-out "what if" scenario can be one of the CEO's most productive management tools.

The next step forward should be putting together a strategic marketing plan for the company.

STRATEGIC MARKETING PLAN

Preparing a strategic marketing plan is really a four-phase project. As we previously observed, all strategy begins with well-defined objectives.

Next comes the operational phase of developing and carrying out the plan. This is followed by measuring the results. The final phase covers the projected financial outcome. In summary, the four phases of the strategic marketing plan are objectives, operations, measurements and financials.

Objectives

- In essence, the objective of the plan is to penetrate a particular market with a specific marketing campaign in order to realize a certain projected outcome.

- The plan should be developed based on the firm's product(s), budget, marketing campaign, competition and time frame.

- A detailed financial projection should be prepared on a monthly basis that sets forth the anticipated marketing results and the projected profitability.

Operations

- The initial step is to determine the market to be penetrated, the message to be conveyed and the media to be employed in reaching the target market.

- The name of the game is generating low-cost qualified leads that turn into sales. Unless the advertising agency is clairvoyant or lucky, it is vital to test market.

- Test marketing should be confined to low-cost strategies such as e-mail or the latest version of pay- per-click or direct mail or even local cable TV.

- Here is a personal example of changing to low-cost strategies. Over the years, I have given a considerable number of seminars. Today, via webinars (seminars on the internet), similar results may be obtained without incurring costly travel, hotels, food, and renting expensive equipment.

- Consider offering incentives such as a "white paper,"— which is a cross between a magazine article and the company's brochure. It is designed to educate a prospective customer by raising a problem and providing a solution involving the company's product. If professionally prepared, it can become an ideal lead-generator and internet download.

- To generate instant credibility for the product, nothing compares to first-class testimonials.

Measurements

- It is critical to track the results of each phase of the marketing campaign in order to determine cost per lead, conversion rate and marketing cost per sale.

- It is important for management to establish benchmarks and measure actual results against these projected targets.

- These benchmarks should be given to the ad agency so they have a yardstick of the company's expectations.

Financials

Here, I'm a little ahead of myself. In a forthcoming chapter, I will cover how to project all operating activities on a month-to-month basis and account for variances between projections and the actual results.

However, prior to launch, you must be aware of the financial feasibility of the marketing campaign as well as the projected profitability.

OK, you have just prepared your first strategic marketing plan. You now know what your objectives are in terms of market penetration, advertising campaign, projected sales volume and profitability. You have decided which low-cost marketing strategy to launch. You also have the benchmarks in place to evaluate performance as events unfold. Sounds like you are on your way.

Now, let's take a brief tour around the world of marketing and summarize what some of the more erudite marketers are saying.

TRADITIONAL MARKETING

Traditional marketing is under attack. First, there is the "advertising is dead" crowd, as represented by Barry Densa (www.writingwithpersonality.com). His thesis is that "consumers have been over-advertised and over-sold" and the only newspaper ads that work are giveaways and going-out-of-business sales. He believes that consumers are desensitized to ads but clamor for information.

David M. Scott offers this insight in *The New Rules of Marketing and PR*, "Traditional marketing is generally so wide and broad that it is ineffective... just does not work for niche products or local services." He questions all forms of non-targeted advertising.

A third critique is presented by J. Walter Smith, Ann Clurman and Craig Wood of the research/polling firm Yankelovich Partners. They authored *Coming to Concurence* and observed that product-centric marketing is failing because 1) knowledgeable customers are less dependent on advertising for information 2) loyal customers can be lost in a mouse click or channel change and 3) messages are beamed daily to a disinterested and turned-off public.

RESEARCH, RESEARCH, RESEARCH

<u>Treasure Hunt</u>

Michael J. Silverstein, and his collaborator John Butman, offer an important insight based on their findings in *Treasure Hunt: Inside the Mind of the New Consumer*. The focus is on interviewing middle-income family buyers and determining how and why they spend their money.

Silverstein offers, "If you spend time listening to consumers…you'll find they have a rationale for every purchase. Their buying decisions are not random; they are predetermined and creatively conceived." Another nugget, "Trading down isn't so much about compromising as it is about rejecting the average for a better product at a lower cost."

Their message is simple enough—listen to your customers and align your marketing strategies accordingly.

<u>Your Gut Is Still Not Smarter than Your Head</u>

Clancy and Krieg followed up the previously mentioned *Counter-Intuitive Marketing* with *Your Gut Is Still Not Smarter than Your Head: How Disciplined, Fact-Based Marketing Can Drive Extraordinary Growth and Profits*.

Here are some of their thoughts:

- Nothing is more important than marketing in determining the success of a business.

- The popular belief that all marketing is seat-of-the-pants is nonsense.

- Too many failing enterprises result from "gut" decisions without upfront relevant research.

- Research can lead to fact-based marketing that can be quantified, tracked and measured.

Professor Don Sexton of Columbia Business School praises the recent edition of Clancy and Krieg's book by noting, "The authors demonstrate forcefully and dramatically with numerous examples—how great, even just good, analysis leads to legendary marketing strategies."

The Must-Have Customer

Robert Gordman and Armin Brott authored *The Must-Have Customer*. Their research focused on discovering the company's core customers. Gordman then opted for having questionnaire responses from core customers—guide the search for must-have customers. Of course, the new breed will share similar attitudes, attributes and values with the core group.

Gordman's basic premise can be seen in his statement, "Trying to decide in the boardroom what's critical to a company without substantial input from core and must-have customers is just plain dangerous. A strategic plan that is internally generated is neither strategic nor a plan."

THE INTERNET

How to Use the Internet

A good place to start is with Bruce C. Brown's *How to Use the Internet to Advertise, Promote and Market Your Business or Web Site with Little or No Money.* It is a great launching pad for the novice as well as a useful refresher course for the more experienced.

Brown attempts to embrace it all. Coverage includes internet advertising, traffic generation, banner ads, Google's AdWords and AdSense, search engine optimization, registering and marketing one's web site, creating e-zines and newsletters, using auto-responders, meta tags, key word settings, pay-per-click and on and on.

Brown's work can serve as both a textbook and reference guide for e-commerce. Not only are all of the above terms readily explained, but they also are presented in a money-making climate.

The danger with "how-to" books is how quickly they become obsolete. This is particularly true in such a rapidly changing media as the internet. The saving grace is that Brown does such a marvelous job of covering the basics that when changes do take place, you will be well grounded to move forward.

The New Rules

David M. Scott takes us along a new pathway in *The New Rules of Marketing and PR.*

He views the internet as the dominant new driving force of marketing—and that it is more about people than technology. He notes that the power of the web flows from the opportunity to engage prospects in conversation and then motivate them to take the desired action.

The key is extraordinary content. Obviously, to motivate buyers with exceptional content, you first must identify your audience and determine what resonates with them. Scott's strategy in reaching this audience is to leverage the use of news releases, blogs, podcasting, viral marketing and social networking.

Web Marketing Concepts

Jerry Bader (www.mrpwebmedia.com) has written a four-page gem for MarketingProfs titled "18 Web Marketing Concepts That Make a Difference."

These 18 creative concepts, individually and collectively, are show stoppers. Bader backs up each concept with hard-hitting and meaningful advice that you can put to use immediately.

From "Think Audiences, Not Markets" to 'Think People, Not Customers" to "Think Emotions, Not Logic" to "Think Communication, Not Copy,"— it is a brilliant summation by someone who has captured the essence of Web marketing. It is a stimulating and important read at:

http://www.marketingprofs.com/7/web-marketing-concepts-that-make-difference-bader.asp

SOCIAL NETWORKING

Writing about Google or Facebook is dangerous to a writer's credibility. Before the ink dries, new apps, services and increased memberships can make the written paragraphs seem like yesterday's news. But, let's give it a try.

GOOGLE

The Google story is hard to believe. The founders, Larry Page and Sergey Brin were both PhD candidates at Stanford University. From $100,000 invested by Sun's co-founder Andy Bechtolsheim in 1998 – and under the guidance of Eric Schmidt and founders - Google today has a capitalization approaching 200 Billion.

It has given the world access to unparalleled information. Google processes over a billion searches daily and controls over 65% of the search engine market. Google's powerhouse advertising programs account for virtually all of its revenue now exceeding 31 Billion.

The new Google + social networking project launched at the mid-point of 2011 is aimed at Facebook. This impressive grouping of real life sharing features should ignite a competitive frenzy leading to cosmic new apps and services. Now, we can safely refer to Google as the search and share engine.

FACEBOOK

The only improbable and unimaginable growth to rival Google is Facebook. How could Mark Zuckerberg in 2004 with three computer science roommates at Harvard – launch an organization that now has some 750,000 active members worldwide? Over 40% of the U.S. population has a Facebook account.

Zuckerberg is a firm believer in the revenue potential in online sharing of video communication, entertainment and marketing. He is marching forward with Microsoft-owned Skype on visual calling and messaging. Netflix seems next since its CEO Reed Hastings resides on Facebook's board

With ¾ billion membership - video advertising and e-commerce cannot lag far behind. If Mark Zuckenberg's current strategy remains on course, Facebook will be well positioned to generate gargantuan-sized revenue and capitalization.

LINKEDIN

LinkedIn is a business-oriented social networking site launched in 2003 by founder Reid Hoffman and others. The current CEO is Jeff Weiner.

It has over 100 million registered users in some 200 countries. Members create an online professional profile that can lead to business contacts, job searches and prospective clients.

TWITTER

Launched in 2006 by Jack Dorsey, Twitter combines social networking and messaging via "microblogging." The messages, called tweets, are limited to 140 characters.

With over 200 million users, it has become a marketing bonanza for politicians, celebrities and now businesses. Its relevancy skyrocketed when used as a news outlet by Iranian protestors.

SOFTWARE IN THE CLOUDS

Some years ago, Sam Palmisano, CEO of IBM, told a gathering of top company officials that one day computing power would be offered on an "as used basis"—similar to the way electrical power is provided.

Yesterday's projection is now today's reality. Why should a company incur the capital costs of hardware and software installation, time and personnel, maintenance and replacement, security and space—when the organization is not using "all that stuff" 24/7?

CLOUD COMPUTING

Let us understand the concept of cloud computing. Previously, if you wanted to perform word processing, you had to install the right software application on your computer. Today, cloud service providers can offer the same software application- that your browser can fully execute - without having to install the software on your computer.

These service providers host enormous computing power and storage on centralized servers. As long as your desktop, laptop, pad computer or smart phone has a web browser – you can access the cloud host.

DIRECT RESPONSE MARKETING

True confession: I have enjoyed considerable success with direct response marketing (DRM). My initial attraction was the low-cost and quick results. You either get a response or make a sale or you don't.

Examples range from direct mail to e-mail campaigns and all marketing activities that call for the prospect to take immediate action. The response can be by phone, mail, credit card, or driving the prospect to your web site. The DRM campaign can appear in all media outlets from newspapers to magazines to radio to TV to the internet.

DRM is not interested in creating imagery, remembrance or brand building. The only concern is qualified responses. If successful, it can be a fast generator of cash flow. In addition, DRM is ideal for inexpensively test marketing the headline, message and media.

DRM enables the smaller firm to compete like the big boys. Here are a few DRM guidelines.

Direct mail and e-mail campaigns are totally dependent on the content of the message and the quality of the lists. E-mails, of course, must employ opt-in lists to avoid spamming. Most mailings should include testimonials, free bonuses, money-back guarantees and payment options.

Google and other search engines offer multiple DRM opportunities ranging from pay-per-click to pay-per-close. Business opportunities on the internet are taking place at a revolutionary pace and you must act diligently to keep informed. However, remember to apply the same caveat and deal only with professionals who are sophisticated in these initiatives. In the long run, they'll pay for themselves.

Audio and video CDs are playing an increasing role in DRM as enclosures in direct mail campaigns, bonus gifts and teaching devices. Audio CDs are relatively inexpensive and can be a major influence in getting the message across.

Kennedy and Joyner

Let me suggest a visit to two old pros in the field of DRM. The first is Dan Kennedy, who can be reached at www.dankennedy.com. The Kennedy organization and allied associates cover DRM from copy to closing. You will be overwhelmed with the content of his site. Kennedy has written extensively including the *BusinessWeek* best-seller, *No B.S. Business Success* as well as *The Ultimate Marketing Plan* and *The Ultimate Sales Letter.*

Next is Mark Joyner, who has produced a winner in *The Irresistible Offer: How to Sell Your Product or Service in 3 Seconds or Less.* The "irresistible offer" is a three-part formula that enables you to instantly capture your prospect with a great slogan. You will learn what it takes to craft a wining offer. The second half of the book is web-oriented an area where Joyner has enjoyed extraordinary success. *The Irresistible Offer* will make DRM come alive for you.

FUTURE THOUGHTS

Watch This

David Verklin and Bernice Kanner have co-authored, *Watch This, Listen Up, Click Here.* They claim that technology is the driving force in changing all phases of advertising from ad creation to media buying to tracking and measuring results.

Consumers will control which information or entertainment is to be delivered and at what time. Web-based technology covering videos, blogs, iPods, MP3s, BlackBerries and cell phones have replaced interruptive marketing. The authors also predict that the "third screen" (mobile phones) will soon rival the other two screens (TV and computers) for customer attention.

Technology also has exploded the media options on all three screens and elsewhere. Therefore, creative marketing will lose its impact if not placed in specialized media catering to the target audience.

The Next 50 Years

Jeffrey Goldfarb wrote a revealing article for American Advertising, *Forecasting the Future—Industry Leaders Predict What's In the Cards for the Next 50 Years in Advertising.*

Here are some revelations,

By 2050, whites will barely exceed 50% of the population. Thus, there is a significant need to market to minorities and immigrants. Just consider the reality that salsa has now bypassed ketchup as the country's leading condiment.

The census projections are that by 2050, the population for these age groups will be:

>18 to 34—86 million
>56 to 64—64 million
>over 65—79 million

Companies cannot continue to market to the over-55 crowd with the same message beamed at 25-year-olds.

Michael Bevan of Toyota sums up advertising's greatest challenge this way: "As big and as powerful and as dynamic as Toyota can be when we launch a campaign and dominate the airways, we are still less than one-fifth of 1 percent of the advertising out there." He adds, "How do we break through that clutter?"

SOME PERSONAL OBSERVATIONS

We must recognize that today's technology has the capacity to compile personal data far beyond name, address, ZIP code and phone number. Every time we buy a book on the internet, seek online information or engage in any form of web communication, data about us can be gathered into a centralized file and a consumer profile emerges.

Assume you visit a site selling solar panels or buy a book on global warming or join a discussion on melting icebergs—you are immediately a prime candidate for firms marketing "green products." You have become a member of a "defined universe."

However, technology that has this capability to compile and profile is only half the story. "Netizens" (citizens who use the internet) form the other half of the equation. When asked to choose between paid content vs. free content burdened with ads—netizens opt for free content.

This general trend will have a four-fold consequence 1) enhancing free content will induce greater web participation 2) every netizen will become profiled into one or more defined universes 3) market-savvy advertisers will proliferate on the web and 4) as netizens, we will trade privacy for greater open content. Time will tell who got the better deal.

My personal timeline for measuring most events related to technology has been governed by Moore's law. Gordon Moore was the co-founder of Intel, the giant computer-chip maker. He predicted, in common parlance, that computer power would double every two years.

At the rate I now see changes unfolding, the future may not be decades away or even according to Moore's two-year time frame. The future it appears may be the day after tomorrow.

THE BEST $800 I EVER SPENT

We have covered a lot of ground in our discourse on marketing. I particularly want you to grasp the full meaning and impact of the three M's of *Market*Message*Media.

For those who may not be "marketing aficionados," it is easy enough to understand the first two M's. After all, if a company is going to advertise, it needs a market to focus on and an inspiring message to attract the audience.

Not enough homage, however, is paid to Media—probably because there are so many options. A company can convey its message in newspapers, magazines, TV, radio, the internet, direct mail and other outlets. But that's the rub. Which is the right one? A great ad with a great product and a great message will surely fail if the selected media does not cater to the target market.

On the other hand, creative media selection can be a bonanza.

I once placed an $800 ad in a highly specialized magazine. There were not many responses. However, one reply came from an executive of a major corporation. This particular chap had been working with a competitor without satisfaction.

As a courtesy for responding to the ad, I offered to analyze the competitor's product at no cost and report back. Three days later, I submitted a professional and comprehensive review. The executive apparently was impressed and called for a one-on-one meeting.

Two weeks after the meeting, their first order arrived. It became a lot easier to close new prospects once they learned my firm was now doing business with—General Electric.

THE WRAP-UP

Let's see what we have gained from our mission in marketing:

- No company can reach its full growth potential without a market-focused management.

- "We believe most strategic planning issues are fundamentally marketing decisions."

- The three M's of *Market*Message*Media are the who, what and where of marketing.

- In test marketing, consider low-cost strategies such as e-mail, pay-per-click, direct mail or even local cable TV.

- The "what if" scenario can be one of the CEO's most productive management tools.

- The strategic marketing plan should be prepared based on the firm's product, budget, marketing campaign, competition and time frame.

- For many SMEs, traditional advertising may be too costly due to a large percentage of the audience being non-prospects.

- A "white paper" can be an ideal lead-generator as an internet "download."

- Although risky, the success stories are multiplying of companies who have reached out to customers for their insight on various social networking sites.

- Benchmarks should be given to agencies as a yardstick of the company's expectations.

- "Traditional advertising is generally so wide and broad that it is ineffective—just does not work for niche products or local services."

- Research can lead to fact-based marketing that can be quantified, tracked and measured.

- Survey responses from core customers serve as the finest research available in attracting must-have customers.

- "A strategic plan that is internally generated is neither strategic nor a plan."

- Many view the internet as the dominant new driving force of marketing—and the key is extraordinary content together with the opportunity to engage the prospect.

- Four social networking sites that have exploded in membership are Google, Facebook, LinkedIn and Twitter.

- The concept underlying social networking sites is building relationships and not the hawking of commercial products.

- Although individual blogs may lack credibility—however, in aggregate—they may be a powerful force in forecasting new trends.

- "Cloud computing" is a reality and some firms are now paying for computing power on an "as-used basis" similar to the billing of electrical power.

- Direct response marketing is not interested in brand building—just qualified responses.

- DRM is ideal for inexpensively test marketing the headline, message and media.

- Direct mail and e-mail campaigns are totally dependent on the content of the message and the quality of the list.

- Technology can be the driving force in changing all phases of advertising—from ad creation, to media buying to tracking and measuring results.

- The "third screen" of mobile phones should soon rival the other two screens (TV and computers) for customer attention.

- Creative advertising will require the placement of ads in specialized media that caters to the targeted audience.

Sooner or later, all marketing transactions must be translated into numbers. Understanding the language of numbers is the topic for our next chapter as we go about "Unlocking the Secrets of Financials."

This page intentionally left blank.

CHAPTER 4

UNLOCKING THE SECRETS OF FINANCIALS

THE BIG THREE

"Profit or Perish" is one of the major themes of our book and I cannot overemphasize its importance.

Yet I have encountered high-minded consultants, commanding extraordinary fees from Fortune 500 companies, who relegate accounting and finance to the realm of "bean counting." Such self-serving smugness is sheer stupidity.

Every business, large or small, needs to earn a profit and generate cash flow to stay alive. Of course, some larger organizations can sustain yearly losses and still meet their obligations via bank borrowings, added capital from investors or the sale of a subsidiary. Even this has its limitations as the company soon becomes a take-over target or a candidate for court protective bankruptcy.

For small and medium-sized enterprises (SMEs), the duality of profits and cash flow are the key life-sustaining organs of the organization.

In the real world, all company transactions are expressed in the financial language of numbers. The format for presenting these numbers centers around the big three financial statements—the Balance Sheet, Income Statement (also called Profit & Loss Statement) and Statement of Cash Flows. Why are these statements so critical?

First, you cannot run a successful business without knowing—

- what you own, owe out and are worth

- whether you are earning or losing money

- if there is sufficient cash on hand to meet next week's payroll

Second, there are other concerned parties who want to know the firm's financial status such as banks, investors, Wall Street, the SEC and the IRS. Further, keep in mind that accountants are the scorekeepers and the "good guys" who prepare these statements according to Generally Accepted Accounting Principles (GAAP).

I will cover the fundamentals of each statement and provide an explanation of how to interpret the resulting numbers. You need not know bookkeeping or debits and credits to follow along. Do I hear a sigh of relief?

Let's begin our financial journey with the Balance Sheet also known as the Statement of Financial Condition.

BALANCE SHEET

The Balance Sheet sets forth the financial position of a company as of a specific date such as December 31, 20XX. Virtually every treatise on the Balance Sheet begins with the formula, Assets = Liabilities + Stockholders Equity

Immediately, most folks without a background in accounting or bookkeeping are lost. Here is a better way to grasp the overall meaning of the Balance Sheet.

All the "stuff" the company owns are called Assets. All the obligations the company owes out are referred to as Liabilities. If we add up all the Assets and then deduct all the Liabilities, we will arrive at the Stockholders Equity. In others words, it is equally true that Assets - Liabilities = Stockholders Equity.

ASSETS

When a company has cash in the bank or any other asset that can be converted into cash or used within a year's time—such as marketable securities, accounts receivable, inventory, notes receivable, prepaid expenses etc.—they are listed as…………………………………...…………..CURRENT ASSETS

When a company owns property that has a lifespan or business use exceeding one year—such as land, buildings, machinery, automobiles etc.—they are presented at original cost less any depreciation and are listed as……………..…..…..FIXED ASSETS

When a company spends money for which there is a continuous benefit—such as deposits with utilities, investment in subsidiaries etc.—they are listed as………….…OTHER ASSETS

LIABILITIES

Company obligations that will mature or need to be paid off within one year—such as accounts payable, taxes payable, accrued expenses etc.—are listed as……………………………………….. …………………………………...…………..CURRENT LIABILITIES

Obligations that are due and payable beyond a one-year period—such as mortgages, bank loans etc.—are listed as…….. ………………………………………..…FIXED LIABILITIES

Special reserves to cover contingencies for which the company may be liable—such as from lawsuits, guarantees, warranties etc.—are listed as …………..…………..OTHER LIABILITIES

STOCKHOLDERS EQUITY

Capital funds contributed by investors plus Retained Earnings (accumulated earnings minus dividends paid out) are listed as……………………………...…..STOCKHOLDERS EQUITY

Now, let's view how a Balance Sheet might be presented for a hypothetical XYZ Corporation.

.

XYZ CORPORATION
BALANCE SHEET
DECEMBER 31, 20XX

ASSETS

CURRENT ASSETS			
Cash		$2,000,000	
Marketable Securities		1,000,000	
Accounts Receivable		3,000,000	
Inventory		4,000,000	
Prepaid Interest and Insurance		500,000	
Total Current Assets			$10,500,000
FIXED ASSETS			
Land		$3,000,000	
Buildings	$10,500,000		
Less Accumulated Depreciation	4,500,000	6,000,000	
Total Fixed Assets			9,000,000
OTHER ASSETS			
Deposits with Utilities			500,000
TOTAL ASSETS			$20,000,000

LIABILITIES

CURRENT LIABILITIES			
Accounts Payable		$1,500,000	
Accrued Expenses		2,500,000	
Note Payable		1,000,000	
Taxes Payable		500,000	
Total Current Liabilities			$5,500,000
FIXED LIABILITIES			
Notes Payable—Long Term			6,000,000
TOTAL LIABILITIES			$11,500,000

STOCKHOLDERS EQUITY

Stockholders Invested Capital	$6,000,000	
Retained Earnings	2,500,000	
Total Stockholders Equity		8,500,000
TOTAL LIABILITIES AND STOCKHOLDERS EQUITY		$20,000,000

Here are some essential clarifications to the Balance Sheet.

1. The Balance Sheet is always prepared as of the last day of the Income Statement. Therefore, if the Income Statement is for the year ending December 31, 20XX, the date of the Balance Sheet will be December 31, 20XX.

2. Be aware that the financial statements may take weeks, even months, to prepare and the financial condition of the company may have materially changed in the interim.

3. The "Footnotes" attached to the Balance Sheet are of paramount importance and should be carefully reviewed.

4. Companies do not normally list on the Balance Sheet such Intangible Assets as patents, or R & D expenditures. Instead, they review such assets in the accompanying Footnotes. However, should the organization purchase another company and pay in excess of that firm's current value—such excess payment is considered Goodwill and will be listed on the Balance Sheet. Some Intangible Assets have enormous value—just consider what the brand name Coca Cola is worth.

5. Many companies do not list Contingent Liabilities on the Balance Sheet, but fully account for them in the Footnotes. For example, what if the company is the defendant in a lawsuit and a negative verdict could potentially render the firm insolvent? Certainly, this contingency is vitally important and must be disclosed.

6. There are two terms which you may not be familiar with—Prepaid Expenses listed in Current Assets and Accruals listed in Current Liabilities. Prepayments are expenses paid in advance that will benefit a future period and include such items as rent, interest and insurance. Accruals are expense that have been incurred but not paid as of the date of the Balance Sheet. Accruals normally cover such expenses as wages, utility bills, supplies and property taxes.

7. Financial analysts often use "ratios" to get a quick evaluation of the Balance Sheet. The most commonly used is called the Current Ratio—which is determined by having the Current Assets divided by the Current Liabilities. The target is a ratio of 2 to1— which means there should be twice as many Current Assets as Current Liabilities. This would indicate that there are sufficient liquid funds on hand to meet the company's short-term obligations.

8. The term "book value" simply refers to the value shown on the Balance Sheet. The "book value" of assets is not to be confused with outside market value or replacement cost. The "book value" of Stockholders Equity also is not the same as market value or what a prospective purchaser would be willing to pay for the enterprise.

INCOME STATEMENT

While the Balance Sheet presents the financial position of the company as of a given date, the Income Statement sets forth the profit or loss the company has experienced over a specific period of time. For example, "For the Year Ended December 31, 20XX" or "For the Quarter Ending March 31, 20XX."

In essence, the basic function of the Income Statement is to match income and expenses and arrive at the Net Income for the period.

Keep in mind that the two statements are interrelated and every transaction on the Income Statement eventually will be reflected on the Balance Sheet. In the simplest of examples, every sale either should add to the cash position or, if charged, increase the Accounts Receivable.

Here is a condensed Income Statement for the hypothetical XYZ Corporation.

XYZ CORPORATION
INCOME STATEMENT
FOR YEAR ENDING DECEMBER 31, 20XX

Sales	$30,000,000
Less Reserve for Returned Merchandise	1,000,000
Net Sales	$29,000,000
Less Cost of Goods Sold	16,000,000
Gross Profit	$13,000,000
Less Operating Expenses	9,000,000
Operating Income	$ 4,000,000
Less Interest	500,000
Pre-Tax Income	$3,500,000
Less Income Tax	1,200,000
Net Income	$2,300,000

There are a number of Income Statement "basics" you should know:

1. Sales are generally listed as a single figure in virtually all Income Statements released to the general public. For internal presentations, sales can be listed by product lines.

2. An excessively high Reserve for Returned Merchandise can be a signal to management that (a) there are quality control problems (b) the product is ineffective and not performing (c) marketing is over-promising and buyers

are disappointed (d) competitors have come out with a better product or have reduced prices and (e) the return policy is too liberal and encourages returns.

3. The Cost of Goods Sold will vary depending on whether the firm is manufacturing the product, buying the product for resale or rendering a service. In a manufacturing company, the Cost of Goods Sold would incorporate the cost of labor, supplies and applicable overhead.

4. The Gross Profit is critically important and is a key figure to be compared to industry benchmarks and year-over-year performance. A significant drop in the Gross Profit normally produces a loss for the period.

5. Operating Expenses feature a variety of expenditures such as salaries, rent, office supplies, telephone, utilities, advertising, legal, accounting, insurance and depreciation charges. Comparing these expenses to prior periods and accounting for the variances is an essential strategy for controlling costs.

6. There are two classifications of expenses—variable and fixed. Variable expenses are those that are incurred every time a sale takes place. Fixed expenses, as the name implies, pretty much remain the same regardless of volume (think rent).

7. In the event an extraordinary cost is incurred such as the loss of a major lawsuit—this cost is listed in a new section titled "Non-Recurring Costs" and is deducted from Operating Income.

8. By the same token, should the company win a major lawsuit—this windfall would be listed in a new section titled "Non-Recurring Income" and be added to Operating Income.

9. Interest and Taxes—once these two non-operating costs are deducted from Operating Income, we arrive at Net Income for the period. It is common practice inside the company to also refer to Net Income as Net Profit.

STATEMENT OF CASH FLOWS

The Statement of Cash Flows compares the company's cash receipts and disbursements so as to arrive at the net cash produced during the period.

The first thing to recognize is that Net Income is *not* the same as Cash Flow. In fact, a company with a profitable Income Statement but with inept cash management—could become insolvent and a candidate for bankruptcy.

The accounting profession's governing board has directed that the Statement of Cash Flows be presented according to these three classifications:

• Cash Flow from Operating Activities

• Cash Flow from Investing Activities

• Cash Flow from Financing Activities

The Statement of Cash Flows can be complicated and difficult to prepare. Fret not. All this falls into the accountants' laps.

They are aided by numerous cash-flow software packages offered by the likes of Intuit Quick Books, Microsoft, Lotus1-2-3 and SAP.

For our purposes, the Statement of Cash Flows is designed to advise management how much cash flow was generated for the period and from where it came—operating, investing or financing.

It is now time to take a senior view into the real world of financial statements.

GAPS IN THE GAAP

In 1973, the Financial Accounting Standards Board was established and the regulations for Generally Accepted Accounting Principles (GAAP) were set in motion. One of the basic problems is that GAAP rules are highly flexible. In fact, the regulations covering GAAP exceed 1000 pages and are subject to numerous interpretations and modifications.

Let's try a "what if" scenario. "What if" you are considering a first-time investment in a company and are given the three financial statements.

After digesting the statements, will you have sufficient information to make a creditable decision? Possibly—but possibly not. Much of the information presented in the statements reflects management's assumptions, estimates, judgments and adjustments applied to the raw financial data.

It should also be noted that accounting adjustments can vary widely and still conform to GAAP standards. Working with identical sets of raw financial data—and following GAAP regulations to the letter—it is possible to produce either a profit or a loss.

Does this mean that financial statements are worthless or fraudulent? Of course not! Yes, there are the likes of Enron, WorldCom, Tyco, and Adelphia, but they are the exceptions.

What I am getting at is simply this. Unless you know—or can question—how various accounts were modified, you must rely on the integrity of management and the certification of the CPA firm to ensure the validity of the statements.

MASSAGING THE NUMBERS

By massaging the numbers, I am not referring to fraudulent behavior such as off-the-books transactions or valuing assets that do not have market value. I am referring to the vast options that management has to assume, estimate, judge and adjust asset and liability values as well as operating activities.

This will become clearer as we highlight how various Balance Sheet components can be valued.

Marketable Securities: This asset is normally listed at cost. However, in a major stock market decline, the underlying shares may be worth only 60% of the original purchase price. In a rising market, the securities could have doubled in value. In either event, significant changes should be disclosed in the Footnotes.

Accounts Receivable: Is the stated amount valid? Are all the accounts current and collectable? Or, do a third of the accounts represent prior year's receivables and are being carried forward year to year? Is the reserve for bad debts (uncollectables) adequate and based on historic norms?

Inventory: This too requires greater clarification. Did the firm employ FIFO (first-in first-out) or LIFO (last-in first-out) in valuing inventory? Does the inventory contain the prior year's merchandise which is out-of-fashion and not saleable? Or, how much of the inventory is obsolete or near worthless due to a competitor's disruptive product line?

Land: Standard practice is to record land at cost. Again, we face the unknown. Has the property skyrocketed in value? Or, has the neighborhood fallen on hard times and land prices plummeted? Without an appraised current value in the Footnotes, there is no way of telling.

Building: Everything stated about land is applicable here. However, we now encounter the deduction for accumulated depreciation. Question—Was depreciation based on industry standards or IRS rules or prior experience with similar buildings? Is the net depreciated value shown on the Balance Sheet comparable to current appraised value or replacement cost?

Accounts Payable and Accrued Expenses: Has the company recorded all invoices for supplies and inventory? Has the company picked up all expenses incurred but not paid as of the Balance Sheet date?

Even with this cursory review, I believe you get the message. Senior-level thinking demands an inquiring mind as to how the account balances were determined.

Finally, any time you encounter statements without appropriate footnote disclosures, you should be on the alert for potentially questionable practices.

NO FAIRY TALES

A reading of the last few pages might seem to indicate that financial statements are the sanctuary for manipulative management.

Not so! What has just been presented lays at the very core of my beliefs—that knowledge leads to understanding.

One cannot possibly arrive at a company's worth or profitability without grasping an understanding of the organization's financial statements. They are the very embodiment, in dollars and cents, of the firm's value and income-producing capability.

I just wanted you to know how best to read them so you don't end up reading a fairy tale.

THE WRAP-UP

Let's recap what we have discovered in unlocking the secrets of financials.

- The duality of profits and cash flow are the life-sustaining organs of the organization.

- You cannot run a successful business without knowing what you own, owe out and are worth—as well as knowing if you are profitable or have enough cash to meet payroll.

- CPAs prepare financial statements according to Generally Accepted Accounting Principles (GAAP).

- Understanding the Balance Sheet lies in the formula, Assets – Liabilities = Stockholders Equity.

- One year is the dividing line between Current and Fixed Assets—same with Liabilities.

- The Balance Sheet presents the financial position of the company as of a given date while the Income Statement matches income and expenses over a specific time period.

- Stockholders Equity reflects the investor's capital contributions plus retained earnings.

- Footnotes are of paramount importance and should be critically reviewed.

- Intangible Assets and Contingent Liabilities having significant value must be recognized in the Balance Sheet or Footnotes.

- Goodwill generally represents the excess payment by the company in acquiring a subsidiary.

- The Current Ratio (dividing current assets by current liabilities) indicates the company's ability to meet short-term obligations.

- "Book value" relates to Balance Sheet valuations and is not to be confused with outside market value.

- Excessive returned merchandise indicates problems ranging from lack of quality control to the failure to match competitive products and prices.

- Gross Profit is a key indicator. A significant drop normally produces a loss for the period.

- Variable expenses are tied to sales. Fixed expenses pretty much remain the same regardless of volume (think rent).

- Extraordinary costs or windfall income (such as lawsuits) should be reported in the Income Statement and also highlighted in the Footnotes.

- Net income is not the same as Cash Flow. There are numerous adjustments to Net Income to arrive at Cash Flow.

- Inept cash management can lead to insolvency even if a company is profitable.

- There are gaps in GAAP because the rules are flexible and subject to various interpretations.

- Financial statements reflect management's assumptions, estimates, judgments and adjustments to the raw financial data.

- The treatment of accounting adjustments can lead to either a profit or loss—and still conform to GAAP rules.

- The integrity of management and the certification of the CPA promote the validity of the financial statements.

- Significant changes to assets which are listed "at cost" on the Balance Sheet should be disclosed in the Footnotes.

- Preparation of financial statements is not an exact science and the omission of Footnotes should put you on alert for potentially questionable practices.

Now that you have grasped an understanding of strategy, customers, marketing and financial statements, it is time to discover the art of management and one great CEO strategy.

This page intentionally left blank.

CHAPTER 5
THE ART OF MANAGEMENT

THE CEO CHALLENGE

This chapter will place you at the center of CEO decision-making.

First, we will uncover the great operating strategy for CEOs. Then, we will go on a panoramic tour and discover what our learned colleagues have to say about management, leadership, and CEO attributes. We will conclude with "The CEO Imperative," offering 30 CEO benchmarks that will guide you to the next level of excellence.

Let's begin.

THE GREAT OPERATING STRATEGY

"What if" you are suddenly appointed CEO of a mid-sized company? You come in without any prior knowledge of the enterprise. You jump in with both feet and soon gain a comprehensive understanding of the company's people, products and cash position.

Because you are an experienced CEO, you immediately direct the accounting department to prepare a Projected Operating Statement for the next 12 months. The projection will be set up on a monthly basis and every member of the management team will participate and be held accountable for his or her contribution.

Assume the first month of the projected operating plan has elapsed. Now, you immediately institute the great four-step operating strategy.

Step 1: Project … yearly operations on a monthly basis (already done)

Step 2: Compare … the actual monthly results to the projection

Step 3: Account … for variances (differences) between actual results and the projection

Step 4: Execute … any required changes

This strategy holds true whether you are dealing with a start-up, SME, subsidiary or the mother company. You project, you compare, you account for variances and you execute any required changes. It is the highest form of managerial accountability.

It does not matter if the initial monthly projections are "guesstimates." I can assure you that by the third month of accounting for variances, you will know more about the company than you ever imagined.

Recall *The Strategy Paradox,* where author Michael Raynor raised the concern that projections made today will vary with tomorrow's changing circumstances. Thus, forecasts are never totally accurate and this results in "strategic uncertainty."

Because our projections are confined to a one-year time frame, the four-step operating strategy will reduce the risk of uncertainty via monthly accountability.

I have personally employed this four-step operating strategy in numerous enterprises with outstanding results. It has never failed. I strongly urge you to adopt this senior approach to management.

Now, let's take a brief tour of management and discover what some of our learned colleagues are saying.

SUSTAINING SUCCESS

There is a plethora of highly rated authors, consultants and assorted gurus who write books that glamorize successful companies. Generally, these case studies are in tune with the writer's pet business theory.

Upon further investigation, it is often found that many of these companies have failed or are in dire straits. The "experts" simply did not recognize that the firms they promoted had limited strategies for sustaining success. As examples:

In the 1980s, the most dominant and influential management book was *In Search of Excellence* by Tom Peters and Robert Waterman. It has been reported—for some time now—that about two-thirds of the firms highlighted turned out to be failures.

In the 1990s, *Reengineering the Corporation* by Michael Hammer and James Champy was the rage. It took a militaristic approach to change as evidenced by its subtitle, *A Manifesto for Business Revolution.* Interestingly, Professor Tom Davenport revealed in *The Fad That People Forgot* that few of the companies that were case studies in *Reengineering the Corporation* have experienced sustained success.

Also in the 1990s, Gary Hamel and C.K. Prahalad wrote *Competing for the Future*, in which two of the promoted firms were Enron and Global Crossing. Likewise, in this first decade of the 2000s, it has been reported that some of the companies in *Good to Great* by Jim Collins are floundering.

All this begs the question, "Why do some great companies fail to sustain a level of success?"

FAILURE TO RESPOND

There are numerous reasons why flourishing companies start to decline, but after considerable research, I have come to the conclusion that the primary cause lies in the "failure to respond to a changing environment."

Why the failure? Well, that depends on where one researches for answers. In *The Self-Destructive Habits of Good Companies*, author Jagdish Sheth lists seven managerial failings ranging from denial to complacency to competitive myopia. In *How,* author Dov Seidman presents views ranging from blind determination to short-term outlook to holding limited beliefs to taking the path of least resistance.

I acknowledge the assessments of these learned authors. However, I also am of the opinion that the causes for "failure to respond to a changing environment" lay both inside and outside the company.

As for inside the company, I am again reminded of Lewis Platt's classic warning: "The single biggest problem in business is staying with your previously successful business model…one year too long."

As for outside the company, we can gain some insight from the landmark book by Harvard professor, Clayton Christensen titled, *The Innovator's Dilemma.* There he describes how great companies can become candidates for failure due to the emergence of a competitive company's "disruptive technology."

I believe all such failings can be overcome—or at least minimized—via awareness and adaptability.

AWARENESS AND ADAPTABILITY

You cannot find the solution if you do not know the problem. This demands awareness.

In mid-size and large enterprises, I advocate the establishment of a team, headed jointly by the vice presidents of marketing and finance. This team will be responsible for issuing a semi-annual report on the status of customer trends, competitive penetration, non-customers, regional and global markets, emerging technologies and all such relevant hard data.

A VP of finance, who is not "just an accountant" but a professional with the skills of a "generalist," can be the ideal partner in accumulating this outside information. In an article for *Forbes,* Peter Drucker concurred and offered, "Developing this data is going to be the next information frontier."

In smaller firms, the CEO and/or staff must commit to religiously getting out in the field and taking the pulse of customers, competitors, impending technologies and prospective new markets. These are the components of both growth and decline and a lack of awareness in these areas invites an inevitable downturn.

As for adaptability, we must recognize that information is meaningless unless acted upon. Therefore, the CEO must build an organization that readily adapts to change. This means an enterprise where flexible strategies can be developed, communicated and soon implemented.

Awareness and adaptability are the hallmarks of a prudent and accomplished CEO.

LEADERSHIP

Let's examine the essence of leadership from multiple perspectives. John Kotter, Harvard professor and world-renown authority on leadership, firmly believes that leaders are made, not born. They need not possess superior intellect or advanced degrees or come from a wealthy family. His two defining attributes are a competitive drive and the capacity for lifelong learning.

In his book *Leading Change,* Kotter describes a number of executives he initially encountered with seemingly ordinary talent. A decade or so later, a subsequent visit revealed a leader of exceptional qualities. He assigns much of this to the power of compounded growth in skills and learning.

Instead of a laundry list of required talents, consider only these two essential components of leadership—risk-taking and resiliency. Without risk taking, a business will stagnate and slowly succumb. Although risk-taking invites failure, the handling of failure can be leadership's finest hour.

The late Steve Ross, former CEO of Time Warner, had an unusual insight into risk-taking and failure. He let it be known, "In this company, you'll be fired for not making a mistake." John Micklethwait published in the *Economist* the ten success secrets of Silicon Valley. One such secret related to the ultimate failure—bankruptcy. Micklethwait wrote, "Bankruptcy is treated like a dueling scar in a Prussian officer's mess." In other words, bankruptcy is displayed like a badge of honor.

Resiliency, the ability to bounce back, is managements answer to challenges, changes, stress and setbacks. In Paul Stoltz's interesting book, *Adversity Quotient,* he proposes that a leader's response to adversity is a global predictor of success or failure.

Competitive drive, lifelong learning, risk-taking and resiliency all point to leadership as a maturing process. This lends further credence to John Kotter's view that leaders are made, not born. There also appears to be a conversion point where a budding leader internalizes "I understand it; I can do it" and starts to gradually usurp the authority to get things done. Just think how little legal authority was initially possessed by Gandhi, Martin Luther King, Jr. or Nelson Mandela.

Now, let us briefly highlight some recent business books reviewing a whole host of desirable CEO attributes.

The Halo Effect by Phil Rosenzweig suggests that all high-performing companies regress over time. The attributes that lead to exceptional accomplishments include leadership, culture, focus, strategy, execution, shrewd judgment, hard work—and a dose of good fortune.

How: Why HOW We Do Anything Means Everything in Business (and in Life) was written by Dov Seidman. As the title implies, "how" a company operates is more important than the products or services offered. In Seidman's leadership framework are the core values of honesty, integrity and justice—and the leadership attributes of vision, communication, appropriating authority, planning and implementing, assuming responsibility and establishing succession.

Bigger Isn't Always Better by Robert Tomasko distinguishes between a "fixer" and a "grower." The "fixer" is the strategist who operates and improves the current enterprise. The "grower" is interested in moving beyond existing boundaries and establishing new and better pathways. Tomasko cites Howard Schulz of Starbucks as a "grower" for selling the public on the experience, rather than on the cup of coffee.

Kiss Theory Good Bye by Bob Prosen is a results-driven treatise that discards theory as being too abstract to achieve desired profitability. Prosen promotes five attributes— superior leadership, sales effectiveness, operational excellence, financial management and customer loyalty. Added to the mix are competitive intelligence, hiring top employees, communicating the vision and installing an accountability-based culture.

The Carrot Principle by Adrian Gostick and Chester Elton is all about recognizing, inspiring and motivating employees for greater performance. In order for such recognition to be effective, management must establish leadership in four areas—goal setting, communication, trust and accountability.

My own favorite books capturing the CEO mind-set are both autobiographical. They include the previously mentioned *Jack: Straight from the Gut* by Jack Welch and *Who Says Elephants Can't Dance?* by Lou Gerstner. With Welch, it began with his vision of every GE subsidiary being No. 1 or No. 2 in every business they were in.

Gerstner's great vision was recognizing that IBM could not remain committed to producing hardware that was fast becoming a commoditized product with low margins. Instead, he turned IBM into a highly profitable software and solution-oriented service company.

Without vision, a CEO is confined to the status quo and that becomes a sure-fire prescription for competitive penetration and an eventual downturn.

THE CEO IMPERATIVE

Because of the significance of the art of management, I will bypass our usual chapter-closing Wrap-up. In its place, I am presenting "The CEO Imperative." These 30 benchmarks can serve as your personal guideline and checklist in managing most any company you are likely to encounter. Some of the suggested benchmarks will be covered in forthcoming chapters.

1. Develop an "enterprise vision" both short and long term.

2. Communicate this corporate "vision" throughout the organization.
3. Make engaging the "right people" a top priority.
4. Expand authority to all knowledge employees—the firm's most valuable asset.
5. Have corporate data stored and accessible to knowledge employees.
6. Encourage co-workers to participate in planning and setting benchmarks.
7. Recognize and reward outstanding employee performance.
8. Introduce and foster an accountability-based operation.
9. Promote ethical behavior as a corporate cornerstone (violation means dismissal).
10. Establish and promote a customer-oriented culture.
11. Create a customer-focused product line.
12. Determine customer profitability—dismiss profit-costing customers.
13. Install technology for responding to customer needs in "real time."
14. Expand "core competencies" to embrace product line requirements.
15. Employ the 15-step strategy in launching new products and upgrading the current line.
16. Continuously research new markets on local, national and global levels.
17. Personally approve all major marketing campaigns.
18. Evaluate all advertising by the three M's of *Market*Message*Media.

19. Know the 12-step "CEO Strategy for Generating New Customers."
20. Recognize that 95% of potential customers may reside outside the USA.
21. Explore going global for greater revenue and profitability.
22. Adopt the mind-set of "Was it better or different—or neither?"
23. Recognize that projections are strategic plans translated into numbers.
24. Manage via accounting for monthly variances and executing required changes.
25. Generate "awareness" via reports on customers, competitors and technology.
26. Recognize that only 29% of innovative ideas come from employees.
27. Realize that great threats and great opportunities lay outside the corporate walls.
28. Become a lifelong learner, risk-taker and be resilient.
29. Be a "grower" and a "fixer"—you can do both.
30. Delegate—you can only do so much with your own two hands.

Never before have corporate leaders needed to know so much about so many issues on so large a scale that will change so often.

CHAPTER 6
INNOVATION

INNOVATION ABOUNDS EVERYWHERE

John Chambers, president of Cisco Systems, recently offered, "If you want to stay competitive, it is important to have the courage to innovate on a continuous basis....you may not be able to predict the future, but you can certainly get the trends right and then innovate to be a leader in any area."

Innovation can be defined as simply the process whereby creative ideas are generated and then converted into viable and profitable products or services.

Where might the creative and innovative ideas come from? Well, according to a PricewaterhouseCoopers study:

- 46%   flowed from customers, suppliers or market intelligence

- 29% originated from employees

- 11% came from consultants and specialists

- 9% came from research and development

- 5% came from competitors

Thus, we can readily observe that innovation is not confined to in-house inspiration alone. Market-savvy CEOs must recognize the significance of innovative ideas generated outside the corporate walls.

Innovation need not be a new, heaven-sent, disruptive product that will overwhelm the competition and dominate the marketplace. It can simply take the form of blending a more attractive design with a more functional usage.

Larger organizations have the added benefit of innovative feedback from customers, trade associations, consultants, academia and the like. However, gathering innovative ideas from customers is still a high priority. They have the greatest knowledge of both the product and the competition.

Smaller firms have the advantage of customer intimacy. The "shoestring strategy" of a well-planned luncheon can provide a stream of creative ideas. Translating such information into innovative products and profits are the distinguishing characteristics of today's successful CEO.

Before leaving this segment, it should be recognized that with only 29% of innovative ideas generated by employees, management must institute incentive programs to encourage greater co-worker participation.

OBSTACLES TO INNOVATION

If the financial benefits of innovation are so well established, why haven't we seen an even greater pursuit of innovative initiatives? The answer lies in the various impediments to innovation, which can be categorized as follows:

1. Some companies are totally focused on cost cutting, outsourcing and just exceeding Wall Street's quarterly numbers.

2. There is an entrenched corporate bureaucracy that opposes any change to the status quo.

3. There is a fear that innovation will disrupt existing business practices because "this is the way we do things around here."

4. Management has not made the financial commitment or formulated the strategy to launch an innovative initiative.

5. Management has not established a compensation plan to reward innovative achievements.

6. Management has failed to assign a senior executive to coordinate the innovative strategy.

7. Management has not made the all-out commitment to change the corporate culture.

Joe Tucci, the CEO of EMC, summed it up convincingly in an article titled "The Role of the CEO in Innovation"—"You can't adapt to the future if you are unwilling to let go of the past."

HOW THE INNOVATIVE PROCESS WORKS

Let's assume that we are dealing with a top-notch management group. It has cut unnecessary waste, outsourced non-core work that can be done better and cheaper elsewhere and has produced industry-leading profit margins.

The CEO recognizes the group is operating in a dynamic marketplace where change is relentless. The CEO now gathers the management team for a day-long conference resulting in the following corporate commitments:

1. In three years, 30% of their revenue will come from products not in the current pipeline.

2. The executive vice president will assume responsibility for the innovative initiative and be accountable for the results.

3. Appropriate funding is approved and the initial financing will be immediately available.

4. The EVP is authorized to engage a top-level innovative consulting firm to help launch the project and guide its implementation.

5. The entire organization will be advised of the commitment via local meetings. Hand-out literature will set forth an attractive reward system for meaningful participation.

6. Management will take the steps to align corporate culture with innovative strategy.

7. Benchmarks will be set up to measure progress at various stages during the three-year period.

In summary form, this is how the innovation process will proceed.

Step 1: The initial thrust will be to encourage ideas and suggestions internally as well as from the marketplace. Every source listed in the PricewaterhouseCoopers study will be contacted and lines of communication established. As the flow of ideas and suggestions arrive, they will be catalogued and a database created.

Step 2: An evaluation team will be formed to review all incoming data. The team will draw upon the experience and expertise of department heads as well as from skilled employees. Software applications will be installed covering the database and evaluation process.

Step 3: This embraces the product development stage. Once an idea or suggestion is selected to be acted upon, it is reality time. Costs must be calculated, production feasibility determined, marketing campaigns formulated and overall profitability assessed.

Step 4: This is the testing and launching stage. Once the product passes the testing phase, a company-wide effort is set in motion to ensure a successful launch.

In essence, this covers the four-step innovation process of 1) creating the database of ideas 2) evaluation and selection 3) product development and 4) test and launch.

The Boston Innovation Group (www.bostoninnovationgroup.com), a major consulting firm in the field, labels its process "Innovation to Cash." The NetCentrics Corporation (www.netcentrics.com) calls its approach "Concept to Cash." It should now be abundantly clear that the function of innovation is to generate new sales revenue and cash flow.

The NetCentrics Corporation offers a suite of software applications that supports all phases of the innovation process.

INNOVATION AND THE ENTREPRENEUR

You might be thinking that innovation may be great for the larger organizations, but what about the small to mid-sized firms where the employees are not the creative types?

How many times have I heard that one?

May I ask you, Mr. or Ms. Entrepreneur, when was the last time you lunched with your top customer or supplier to generate some great new ideas?

"What if" you decided to become innovative and selected just one of your major concerns to get the process started? Next, how about,

> 1) conferring with your employees
> 2) advising them of the problem
> 3) outlining an innovative strategy
> 4) setting forth a compensation plan
> 5) asking for their ideas and suggestions

I can assure you, all employees want to be recognized for their contribution and compensated for their performance.

Today, the CEO of a SME has the tools and technologies to compete with the bigger companies. This enables the CEO to search out niche markets that larger organizations are unaware of or unable to financially compete.

The power of approximately 35 million American SMEs is undeniable. They employ over half the workforce, account for over 50 percent of non-farm GDP and according to the Small Business Administration, produce 55 percent of all new innovation.

The opportunity today for SMEs to innovate is wide open. It just requires a knowledgeable and committed CEO.

THE POWER OF SMALL IDEAS

Alan Robinson and Dean Schroeder co-authored *Ideas Are Free: How the Idea Revolution Is Liberating People and Transforming Organizations.* In a presentation at the Fashion Institute of Technology in New York City, Robinson stressed the need to stay competitive via innovative ideas from front-line employees.

He cited the Dana Corporation, a large Midwestern manufacturing company, where surprisingly—800 interesting suggestions originated from the receptionist. Upon investigation, it was learned that when customers called in with meaningful complaints, she would simply ask, "What would you do about it?"

He summed-up the presentation with, "You need big ideas to stay in the game, but small ideas will put you ahead."

INNOVATION AND THE CUSTOMER

From the outset, I have highlighted the innovative role the customer plays. In the PricewaterhouseCoopers study, it was noted that customers, suppliers and the marketplace contributed 46% of the creative ideas.

Now, a number of innovative strategists are calling for even greater customer participation. Professor Stephen Brown of Arizona State University, along with Stefan Michel and Andrew Gallan, has published an article, "The Customer: An Overlooked Component of the Innovation Process." The authors point out that web sites such as YouTube and Wikipedia would be worthless without customer contributions.

The researchers propose that organizations look to customer input in the development of innovative products or services. They cite the Swiss newspaper *20 Minuten*, which went to a free, shorter version and increased readership when it became a hand-out.

American companies are starting to seek out customer participation in innovative ways. General Motors, via the Chevy Tahoe, invited participants to create and post their own SUV ads online— with Chevy supplying video clips and music. The response was enormous with ads gravitating to YouTube and all over the net.

Of course, such campaigns carry a high risk should participants turn negative. However, the potential is staggering. Just consider an enterprising ad executive, sitting in an ivory tower on Madison Avenue and letting customer-feedback determine the content of future campaigns.

As set forth in Chapter 3, I encourage you to read the article "Social Marketing: How Companies Are Generating Value

from Customer Input," which can be found at
http://knowledge.wharton.upenn.edu/article.cfm?articleid=1864.

Marketing and advertising executives are furiously probing how
to harness the power of the enormous growth of social
networking sites.

INNOVATION AND CUSTOMER SERVICES

One of the most overlooked innovative opportunities lies in
providing greater services to existing and prospective
customers. Just consider,

1. Providing a range of services enhances the company's
    capability to find solutions to customer problems.

2. Furnishing both products and services should ensure
    greater customer loyalty.

3. Penetrating a customer's operation with products and
    services should create a dependency that translates into
    capturing new purchases and replacements.

4. By entering the service field, the company should gain
    the experience to develop a new line of add-on services.

5. New innovative services can become a significant
    source of revenue and cash flow.

We live in a service economy, but our innovative tools and
thinking are not reflective of this reality. Entrepreneurs and
CEOs should take heed of this unique opportunity.

MEASURING INNOVATION

There seems to be a debate in the academic and consulting communities with regard to measuring innovation.

On one hand, there are those who believe in the Wall Street metrics of increased profitability, new products introduced, gains in market share and the like. Then, we find those who prefer measuring innovation on the basis of improved relationships with customers and suppliers.

Another group believes that innovation is largely determined by geography, citing Silicon Valley as proof. When Lewis Platt headed up Hewlett-Packard, he set the tone on innovation when he said, "Obsolete ourselves or the competition will."

My own view is that all the above beliefs are valid. However, we innovate primarily to satisfy the customer and generate added revenue and profits.

THE WRAP-UP

Let's see what we have discovered about innovation.

- Innovating on a continuous basis is the only way to stay competitive.

- 46% of creative ideas come from customers, suppliers and the marketplace—only 29% from employees. Management must encourage greater co-worker participation.

- Innovation need not be a new and disruptive product that will suddenly dominate the marketplace. It can simply be a design and usage change that satisfies the customer.

- The obstacles to innovation may be summarized as 1) corporate bureaucracy opposing any changes 2) fear of disrupting existing business practices 3) failure to assign a responsible executive to oversee the initiative 4) lack of financial funding 5) no plan to reward innovative achievements and (6) no commitment to change corporate culture.

- "You can't adapt to the future if you are unwilling to let go of the past."

- To launch a company's innovative strategy requires 1) establishing realistic targets 2) appointing a senior executive to oversee the process 3) providing necessary financing 4) communicating the innovative strategy effectively and continuously 5) creating the climate for employee participation with appropriate incentive rewards 6) aligning corporate culture with innovative strategy and 7) setting up benchmarks to measure ongoing progress.

- The four steps of the innovation process maybe condensed as 1) creating the database of ideas 2) selecting and evaluating the best 3) product development and 4) testing and launching.

- Integrated software applications are available that cover all phases of the innovative process—comparable to CRM for sales and marketing.

- Entrepreneurs and small-company CEOs can initiate innovation by 1) selecting just one major concern 2) conferring with employees 3) advising them of the problem 4) outlining an innovative strategy 5) setting rewards for reaching targets and 6) asking employees for ideas and suggestions.

- America's 35 million SMEs produce 55 percent of all new innovations.

- 800 suggestions originated from an innovative receptionist who asked customers calling to complain, "What would you do about it?"

- The majority of employee-generated innovative ideas come from employees dealing directly with customers and suppliers.

- Astute marketers are looking to customers as co-creators of innovation on social networking sites. The rewards can be extraordinary, but the risk of a highly publicized rejection can be devastating.

- Introducing innovative "services" can produce exceptional company benefits including 1) enhancing the company's ability to find solutions to the customer's problems 2) ensuring greater customer loyalty 3) affording greater opportunity to capture new purchases and replacements 4) opening the door to develop new lines of services and 5) generating increased revenue and profits.

- We live in a service economy, but our innovative tools and thinking are not reflective of this reality.

- The best benchmarks in measuring innovative success are still customer satisfaction and company profitability.

Now that you are accomplished in the art of innovation, let us delve into the company's product line—for a real surprise.

CHAPTER 7
PRODUCT LINES

A DOZEN THOUGHTS

A chapter on product lines might not seem very exciting so I'll have to add some pizzazz. In fact, I plan to tie together "stuff" we learned in two prior chapters. It should produce "something" you will find exciting and useful.

But first, let's get a feel for products and product lines. "What if" you were just introduced to a company's product line? What thoughts would run through your mind?

- Which products are profitable and which need to be discarded?

- Has any market research been conducted and implemented?

- Do the products satisfy customer needs and solve their problems?

- How does the line compare to competition from price to performance?

- Are the products better or different—or just commodities?

- Can the products be produced or acquired at the "right price"?

- What new features will render the line more attractive, competitive and saleable?

- What percentage of the market does the product control?

- Are there new markets to be opened for expansion?

- How many marketing dollars are needed to maintain current volume?

- Will new marketing strategy generate added revenue?

- Can new "services" be introduced to existing customers?

While pondering these views, let's examine how product lines can serve as the company's growth engine.

PRODUCT LINE STRATEGY

When Arthur Martinez was chairman of Sears, he set the tone for corporate growth with, "You cannot shrink your way to greatness."

Management must recognize that to generate growth, it must arm the company with customer-driven product lines. This means products that can compete in the marketplace because of superior design, performance, technology, reliability, special features, convenience, pricing and service.

Jeremy and Tony Hope, the international consultants co-authored *Competing in the Third Wave*. There, the Hopes outlined management's options in product line strategy as follows, "They (management) understand that they cannot be all things to all people... they choose one of three propositions on which to compete: product leadership, operational excellence or customer intimacy."

As for product leadership, the Hopes cite Microsoft for Windows and Nike for its shoe line. With regard to operational excellence, they highlight Wal-Mart and Dell computers. Customer intimacy relates to those organizations that focus on satisfying the special needs of their customers. The Hopes offer British Airways for catering to executive travelers and Staples for fulfilling the needs of the small business customer.

COMPUTER CHIPS AND POTATO CHIPS

Now "what if" your company has not achieved product leadership or operational excellence or customer intimacy? Then you and/or your staff must get out into the field and determine what it will take to promote product line growth. If need be, bring on consultants, conduct surveys, lunch with top customers—just find solutions!

I do not care whether your company is producing computer chips or potato chips—your product line is your growth engine. Your new product line can be your old product line redesigned and repackaged with improved performance and upgraded services.

Let's face reality. Introducing a totally new product line can be costly. It demands market research, product development, considerable funding, production capabilities, market testing, advertising campaigns and engaging new personnel. This is why my initial approach is always to examine the option of upgrading the current product line.

GUIDELINES IN UPGRADING
EXISTING PRODUCT LINES

Product line strategy embodies one of senior management's major challenges. Not only will profitability be at stake, but in some cases, the very survival of the company. Here is a 15-step guideline for upgrading an existing product line.

1. Establish a realistic vision of what is to be accomplished.

2. Have senior management make a total commitment to upgrade the line.

3. Produce current research of markets, customers, competitors and technology.

4. Promote customer satisfaction as center stage for the strategy.

5. Appoint a senior executive to implement strategy and accept responsibility.

6. Approve funding for the immediate launch of the project.

7. Consult with all department heads in formulating upgrading strategy.

8. Do not restrict the upgrading strategy to existing core competencies or equipment.

9. Clearly define all upgrading processes and procedures.

10. Communicate endlessly so co-workers buy into the upgrading plan.

11. Empower employees to fully participate in determining upgrading strategy.

12. Prepare marketing campaigns for testing and launching.

13. Put in place all benchmarks and measurements.

14. Align corporate culture with the upgrading strategy.

15. Target the upgrading strategy to be completed within six months.

These guidelines will well serve the CEO in implementing the upgrading strategy.

COMMODITIZATION

"What if" you come into a company that is moderately successful but whose management lacks vision and prefers the status quo? What can be the fallout? I am certain you recognize—this is an open invitation to competitors and the onslaught of commoditization.

Commoditization refers to look-alike products with similar performance that enter the marketplace. The competitive edge for newcomers is price cutting—as they generally operate at a lower overhead. For the established company, this could mean a loss of price-conscious customers. The threat can become even graver, should these discounters offer products with a technological advantage.

What are the CEO's options in meeting the challenge of commoditization—beyond "fanatical services" previously reviewed?

1. Customization: In a world of sameness, people want to be treated to personalized services. Technology has

opened the door. Customers can have their jeans custom-fitted at a Gap store. Your home windows can be customized by contacting an Andersen Windows dealer. Burger King promotes "Have it your way." The greater the personalization of a sale, the greater the opportunity to build long-term loyal customers. Customizing a product offering means you are no longer selling a "commodity."

2. Branding: Branding is simply a campaign to stand out in a crowded marketplace by creating a distinctive personality and promoting it relentlessly. Branding requires a company-wide effort in merchandising this "distinctiveness." This includes advertising, public relations, management speeches, corporate imaging, product packaging etc. Companies who have made branding an obsession have enjoyed remarkable results—Coke, McDonald's, Marlboro, IBM, Apple, GM and GE, to mention a few. Branding is also the route to growth from modest beginnings such as experienced by Martha Stewart and Tommy Hilfiger.

3. Design: Great design is more than just being different. It can sustain a product's competitive edge even after technological advantages and product newness fade. Tom Peters makes the case for design's pre-eminence by quoting the late Norio Ohga, Sony's former chairman, "At Sony, we assume all products of our competitors will have basically the same technology, price, performance and features. Design is the only thing that differentiates one product from another in the marketplace." The design culture must not only be reflected in product offerings but in packaging,

111

shopping bags, stationary etc. Design works best when it pleases the senses and is functionally useful. Design brings a "newness" to the customer that outpaces the competition.

4. New Markets: Consider expanding the product line into untapped markets. If the enterprise has not mass-marketed on the internet, then test market USA and global offerings from Google to Baidu—and from e-mail solicitation to pay-per-click.

5. New Products for Old Customers: Explore adding new and allied products that can offer unique solutions to your current base of customers.

6. Sell Services: Be ever mindful of IBM's gigantic turnaround and transition from a hardware company to a software and service enterprise.

LAUNCHING A NEW PRODUCT LINE

I have now covered the essence of product management from creating strategy to upgrading the current line to overcoming commoditization. There is one more race to run.

"What if" you are called upon to launch a new product?

Well, this basically falls into two phases—what to do before the launch and how to manage the operations afterwards. In launching a new product line, just follow the same 15 guidelines just covered in "upgrading" the existing product lines.

Now, let's turn our attention to the post-launch phase. It embodies the "something" that you must grasp in becoming smarter than a CEO. First, let's draw upon the insight of two prior chapters.

In "Financials," you learned that the results of operations for a given period can be expressed in a Profit & Loss Statement (previously referred to as an Income Statement). Then, in "The Art of Management," you discovered the great four-step operating strategy of project, compare, account for variances and execute required changes.

When you put together the dynamic duo of a Profit & Loss Statement and the great four-step operating strategy—you gain a significant understanding of the company. Let's prove it.

For ease of illustration, I'll employ simple numbers. Assume you project $1000 in sales for the first month of the product launch. However, the actual sales come in at only $800. Further, assume all planed advertising was spent, selling expenses dropped slightly due to fewer commissions paid and overhead remained the same. Here is how it would look to you.

	Projected	Actual
Net Sales	$1000	$800
Cost of Goods Sold	350	280
Gross Profit	$650	$520
Operating Expenses		
Marketing – Advertising	80	80
Selling Expense	50	40
Overhead Costs	250	250
Total Operating Expenses	$380	$370
Pre-Tax Operating Profit	$270	$150

Notes:

1. Although sales declined 20% from the projection ($1000 to $800), the pre-tax operating profit dropped almost 44% ($270 to $150).

2. The initial question is why the 20% drop in sales? Did the advertising campaign fail to generate the projected leads? Were the leads unqualified? Was the sales force properly trained to close prospective customers?

3. Note that although actual sales were off by 20%, the launch was profitable. It generated a Pre-tax Operating Profit of 19% ($150 into $800).

These are just the preliminary observations an inquiring CEO should consider.

THE "NAPKIN STRATEGY"

You must—I beg of you—become comfortable with numbers. You need not know how to prepare a Profit & Loss Statement. That's the job of the accountants. However, you must learn to make numbers work for you. Reread the chapter on "Financials" until it all sinks in.

I have personally mapped out many a deal on the dry-side of a cocktail napkin. Here is a ballpark approach to "napkin strategy."

Project some reasonable number for Sales. Then estimate 35% of Sales for the Cost of Goods Sold. This should leave you with a Gross Profit of 65%. Then forecast Marketing at 8%,

Selling Expense at 5% and Overhead Costs at 25%— for Total Operating Expenses of 38%. Thus, you end up with a Pre-Tax Operating Profit of 27% (65% Gross Profit less 38% of Total Operating Expenses). Management will normally give a willing ear to a 27% pre-tax project.

P.S. This is exactly how I projected the Profit & Loss Statement on two prior pages.

The "napkin strategy" presented here is a variation of the formula of 1/3 for Cost of Goods Sold, 1/3 for Operating Expenses and 1/3 for Profit. Certainly, the percentages will vary depending upon the industry being analyzed. It will differ materially if the firm is rendering a service.

"Napkin strategy" is an impressive way to go. Before an important meeting, you can always do a Google or Yahoo search for a particular industry's percentages.

A REMARKABLE CONTRIBUTION

In 1997, Harvard professor Clayton Christensen wrote a remarkable book named, *The Innovator's Dilemma.* Intel's then-chairman, Andrew Grove, described it as "Lucid, analytical—and scary."

Christensen proposed that large corporations—who are leaders in their field, with great product lines, who listen to their customers and who invest in emerging technologies—can still be major candidates for failure. The culprit is an initiative known as "disruptive technology."

By "disruptive technology," Christensen refers to new companies, marketing new products that are cheaper, provide a lower profit margin and appeal to a limited market.

Christensen reviews the effect of "disruptive technology" in various industries, including the most celebrated case of all. That's the one where some small Southern store began selling discounted merchandise in towns with a population smaller than 200,000. That was the initial step in its march to becoming the world's largest retailer—Wal-Mart.

CEOs of firms employing "disruptive technology" have a masterful understanding of the marketplace by way of 1) producing new products that sell 2) locating and entering a low-volume niche market 3) penetrating the customer base of the larger company and 4) earning a profit with lower prices and reduced profit margins.

How does one acquire this know-how? Here's how.

1. Escape the confines of internal corporate thinking

2. Fully engage customers, competitors, suppliers and consultants

3. Become industry savvy—devour trade publications and attend/participate in trade shows

4. Research the net, from Google to blogs, for notable industry data

Simply stated, ingest and digest the marketplace of ideas, products and services.

THE WRAP-UP

It's time to wrap things up and see what we have encountered this time.

- If properly managed, product lines can be the company's growth engine.

- There are a dozen thoughts a CEO should entertain in tackling a new product line: 1) Which products are profitable and which need discarding? 2) Has market research been implemented? 3) Are customers satisfied? 4) How does it compare to competition?
  5) Are the products different or just "commodities?" 6) Can the product be produced at the "right price?" 7) What new features will render the product more saleable? 8) What percent of the market is now controlled? 9) Are there untapped markets? 10) How many marketing dollars are required to maintain current volume? 11) Will a new advertising campaign generate increased revenue? 12) Can new "services" be introduced?

- Look to gain a competitive edge via product leadership (think Microsoft), operational excellence (think Wal-Mart) or customer intimacy (think British Airways).

- Compare upgrading the existing product line vs. introducing a costly new line.

- The 15 guidelines in upgrading an existing product line cover 1) vision 2) management commitment 3) research 4) customer satisfaction 5) senior executive oversight 6) funding 7) department-head participation 8) core competencies 9) processes and procedures 10) co-worker communication 11) employee participation 12) test marketing 13) benchmarks 14) corporate culture and 15) completion in six months.

- Commoditization can be overcome via customization, branding, design, opening untapped markets, new product offerings and introducing new services.
- Launching a new product line requires following the same 15 guidelines as set forth in "upgrading" the existing product line.
- When sales revenue declines, the effect on profit can be dramatic.
- You must become comfortable with numbers and make them work for you. "Napkin strategy" can work wonders (especially after the second martini).
- Senior management is more inclined to approve projects backed by detailed financial data and profitability projections.
- "Disruptive technology" can overtake even the best-managed companies. Therefore, early awareness and adaptability are critical.
- Ingest and digest the marketplace of ideas, products and services in your field. If you have come this far, then you have the capacity to acquire this knowledge.

It is now time to move on to a company's greatest long term asset—its co-workers.

CHAPTER 8
KNOWLEDGE EMPLOYEES
(KEs)

THE THREE QUESTIONS

Employees can make or break a company.

Thus, what guidance can I offer you? Well, I believe it would be best if I start with three penetrating questions.

- What do employees really want?

- What are the barriers to employee empowerment?

- What can the company expect in return?

I suspect many of you are under the impression that all "old-time employee/management relationships" are outdated. That the ongoing changes in technology, globalization and the emergence of knowledge employees (KEs)—have transformed everything. That Gen X has no interest in job security.

Not so. In a Silicon Valley study after the dot-com bust, job security became the number one sought-after benefit.

After researching numerous publications on the employee/management relationship, here are my summarized responses to the three questions. As always, my first objective is to provide you with a broad-based understanding of the topic under review and then move on to practical solutions.

WHAT DO EMPLOYEES REALLY WANT?

- Fair and reasonable compensation

- Other benefits (medical coverage)

- Job security

- Job satisfaction

- Treated with respect

- Recognition for achievements

- Rewarded for accomplishments

- Profit-sharing program

- Company training programs

- Opportunity for advancement

- Participate in planning and strategy

- Engage in local decision making

- Join self-managed teams

- Eliminate downsizing and outsourcing

- Be proud of job and company

- Greater involvement in the company

These provide an admirable array of potential benefits. However, few companies can remain competitive in the global marketplace by offering them all. They are presented here as target benefits and not as a present-day mandate.

WHAT ARE THE BARRIERS TO
EMPLOYEE EMPOWERMENT?

- Financial costs—perceived or real

- Management does not believe in or understand empowerment

- Employees are looked upon as costs, not as partners or assets

- Management does not listen to or respect employees

- Management is incompetent and/or resistant to change

- Management considers wage payment as its prime/sole responsibility

- Management micromanages and counteracts employee decisions

- Management fails to set benchmarks

- Management does not believe in the need for employee recognition, rewards, training, participation in planning or decision making

Some of these barriers, which represent a 19th-century mentality, must be discarded. With the emergence of knowledge employees, a more conciliatory and "partnering" approach is needed. Productivity and profitability are at stake.

WHAT CAN MANAGEMENT
EXPECT IN RETURN?

- Quality performance and continuous improvement

- Employee loyalty and reducing cost of replacement

- Enriched interaction with customer

- Increased submission of innovative ideas

- Team player and getting along with co-workers

- Assume greater responsibility and accountability

- Foster internal cooperation and coordination

- Behave ethically with customers and co-workers

- Refer needed employees

- Source for future company management

- Become a more skilled and valuable asset

- Higher company profits

These expectations are both realistic and obtainable. This is why the employee/management relationship is so important. Coming to terms with employees in this age of knowledgeable co-workers will be one of management's most notable achievements.

With these guidelines, you have the basic foundation to tackle employee/management challenges. Let's take the next step forward and consider treating knowledge employees (KEs) as business people.

KNOWLEDGE EMPLOYEES

A knowledge employee (KE) can be defined as any employee who uses information in the performance of his or her duties. Thus, KEs can be engineers, accountants, researchers, marketers, software programmers, buyers, team leaders, department heads and the like. The recruitment, training, empowerment and motivation of KEs are vital components of an elite management.

As KEs become significant players in determining a company's productivity and profitability, management must be receptive to profit-sharing programs. In *Post-Capitalist Society,* Peter Drucker warned: "In knowledge and service work, however, partnership with the responsible worker is the only way to improve productivity. Nothing else works at all."

Here are some creative examples of how employee participation, empowerment and partnership can work in the "real world."

EVERY EMPLOYEE A BUSINESS PERSON

In *The Circle of Innovation,* Tom Peters advances the concept of turning every employee into a business person. He cites the extraordinary trust the Ritz-Carlton Hotel in San Francisco places in its housekeepers, bellhops, and doormen. Each is authorized to spend up to $2000 to satisfy a customer's complaint.

EMPLOYEES AND OPEN-BOOK MANAGEMENT

One of the more creative approaches to employee empowerment is open-book management (OBM).

It is based on the insight that as co-workers become privy to the company's financial and marketing results, they feel a sense of participation and become more productive. OBM is centered on the following blueprint.

1) Educate employees in the meaning of financial statements.

2) Report financial results openly and often.

3) Train employees to use this information in their decision making.

4) Offer employees participation in the success of their suggestions.

5) Treat employees as stockholders.

Transforming a company to OBM requires a new managerial mind-set. However, companies who have engaged in OBM have been rewarded with employees who are highly motivated to contribute. John Case has two exceptional books on OBM, *The Open-Book Experience: Lessons from Over 100 Companies Who Transformed Themselves* and *Open-Book Management: The Coming Revolution.*

EMPLOYEES AS STRATEGISTS

Stephen and Shannon Wall, a husband-and-wife consulting team, have taken Tom Peter's idea of turning every employee into a business person—to the next level. From a 10-year study of some 200 firms, such as AT&T and 3M, the Walls have formulated an interesting proposal in their book *The New Strategists*. They advocate making employee empowerment a reality by granting co-workers a voice in strategic planning. They believe greater productivity, trust and loyalty will follow.

THE INDIVIDUALIZED CORPORATION

S. Ghoshal, chair of strategic leadership at the London Business School, and Harvard Business School professor C. A. Bartlett have produced an impressive book titled *The Individualized Corporation*. They call upon management to create a culture whereby employees' skills are maximized. They identify three "core capabilities" of the individualized corporation as 1) motivating individual employee creativity 2) coordinating their entrepreneurial talents and 3) revitalizing the organization and its product lines.

In essence, employees are encouraged to generate new ideas and to accept greater accountability for their actions. Management's responsibility is to empower, support and harmonize such activities. Ghoshal and Bartlett point to a number of organizations that have successfully made the transition to greater employee participation such as GE, 3M, Intel and IKEA.

Management must recognize that the participation of KEs and their creativity are the driving forces in the organization remaining competitive and reinventing itself.

For the first time in history, KEs are bringing their own tools to the job site—their brainpower.

EVERY DEPARTMENT A SMALL BUSINESS

Here is an exciting concept.

Often overlooked are the company's service departments. These can include finance, engineering, security, purchasing, legal, marketing, maintenance, shipping and warehousing. These service departments are headed by KEs who possess the largest fund of knowledge covering their local operation. In many cases, they also interface directly with the customer.

If the organization is now delegating authority to KEs—sharing knowledge, educating them in financial statements, creating an entrepreneurial culture, making every KE a business person and rewarding achievements—then why not turn every service department into a small business unit?

The possibilities are compelling.

1. Structuring a service department as a business unit is not difficult. From an accounting viewpoint, it is easy enough to calculate how much of the sales dollar is contributed by each service department. As for expenses, all costs and overhead can be allocated on some equitable basis. A monthly or quarterly Profit & Loss Statement would usher in a whole new meaning to "open-book management." It could pave the way for turning every co-worker into a financially aware business person.

2. The company will be training one of its key KEs— the department head—in understanding the relationship between authority and accountability. Department heads, trained both operationally and financially are a

127

fertile field from which future managers can be selected.

3. These financial numbers also can serve as the basis for performance recognition and profit participation. These are cardinal steps in bringing about employee loyalty and trust.

4. If the department's staff interfaces with customers, then the projected results can be even more dramatic. Recent research confirms that KEs, with a stake in the company's performance, can be invaluable in fulfilling customer satisfaction.

5. Measuring the performance and profitability of a service department also provides management with the hard data against which they can compare the projected cost of outsourcing.

All in all, operating each department as a small business presents the ideal setting to upgrade co-worker skills, develop loyalty and build a competitive edge that few on the outside can match.

DOES "ALL THAT JAZZ" REALLY WORK?

In a recent conference at Emory University in Atlanta, a rather interesting study was presented by Professor Monica Worline. It involved the billing department at a local community hospital.

The department of 30 was overworked and it took an average of 182 days to collect a payment. Management threatened to close the operation if improvements were not forthcoming.

With company support, the team united, camaraderie ensued, resiliency flourished and average collections were reduced to 60 days. In addition, department turnover came down to 1% while the average rate of turnover for the rest of the organization remained considerably higher.

"Small stuff," you might say. However, big business is an aggregate of a lot of "small stuff." The bottom line is simply this—with management's guidance, "all that jazz" about employee participation really does work.

THE VALUE OF HUMAN CAPITAL

Intellectual capital is normally classified as either human or structural capital. Human capital obviously refers to the skills, knowledge, experience, creativity and innovative capabilities of the company's personnel. Structural capital covers patents, trademarks, research papers, manuals, processes, databases, customer lists, software applications and the like.

Thomas Stewart illustrated the value of human capital in his superb book, *Intellectual Capital*. He cites the case of the advertising agency formerly known as Saatchi & Saatchi. When the Board of Directors voted to fire Maurice Saatchi, a number of other executives voluntarily left with him. This was followed by the exodus of some of the firm's most valued clients. Subsequently, the stock price on the NYSE dropped in half. Thus, shareholders lost 50% of their equity when the firm lost its human capital, as represented by Maurice Saatchi and the defecting executives.

Interestingly, the firing of Maurice Saatchi is not a transaction that accountants normally report on the company's Balance Sheet. Yet as illustrated above, the financial consequences to the company and shareholders were rather significant.

If knowledge is not shared within the company, then the enterprise faces the Saatchi dilemma. When executives or KEs leave, they take their human capital with them. Thus, it is imperative to manage a company's human capital so that the loss of a few will not bring harm to the many.

THE WRAP-UP

What have we really harvested in our discussion regarding knowledge employees?

- It all begins with asking the three basic questions: What do employees really want? What are the barriers to employee empowerment? What can the company expect in return?
- For a summarized response to all three questions, review the data presented at the beginning of the chapter.
- Management must recognize that KEs are its most valuable long-term asset and create an environment for constructive employee participation.
- KEs are all co-workers who use information in the performance of their duties.

- The recruitment, training, empowerment and motivation of KEs are telltale signs of an elite management.
- Peter Drucker warned, "Partnership with the responsible worker is the only way to improve productivity."
- Every employee can be a business person. Housekeepers, bellhops and doormen at the Ritz-Carlton were authorized to spend up to $2000 to satisfy a customer's complaint.
- Open-book-management (OBM) promotes a feeling of employee involvement and motivates greater productivity.
- Some consultants now advocate KEs participating in strategic planning.
- For the first time in history, KEs are bringing their own tools to the job site—their brainpower.
- Structuring a service department as a business unit is doable. A quarterly Profit & Loss Statement would give new meaning to open-book-management.
- KEs, with a stake in the company's performance, can be a major asset in fulfilling customer satisfaction.
- With company support, motivated personnel can produce extraordinary results.
- Although not shown by accountants on the Balance Sheet, the loss of a company's human capital can materially affect the company's profitability and stockholders equity.

Now that we have examined the role of knowledge employees, let's peer into the realm of entrepreneurship.

This page intentionally left blank.

CHAPTER 9

ENTREPRENEURSHIP

A GLOBAL AWAKENING

Few terms are as overworked as entrepreneurship. At times, it could embrace the endeavors of Donald Trump. Then again, it could designate the high school girls who wash cars on weekends to fund breast cancer awareness.

However, it is still the appropriate label to describe the estimated 35 million enterprises of the self-employed, home-based business operators, freelancers, independent contractors, temps, professionals, consultants and the like.

This is not just a USA phenomenon. There is an interesting study by Michael Schaper, dean of Murdoch University Business School in Australia. His research of local countries revealed that SMEs constitute some 99% of private-sector firms in Australia, China and Malaysia. New Zealand came in at 97%.

The key underlying cause for this surging growth has been the emergence of technology. The empowerment of the computer, internet and mobile communications has enabled individuals to transact business as never before. I would not be surprised if this entrepreneurial trend is related to the same need for self-expression now exploding in blogs, podcasting and social networking.

OWNER ENTREPRENEUR VS.
CORPORATE ENTREPRENEUR

There are two separate but connected classes of entrepreneurs. The first group refers to the approximately 35 million owner entrepreneurs listed above. The next category covers the

134

corporate entrepreneurs who operate within the confines of the larger companies.

Although they share much in common, they carry distinctive burdens. The owners take on the multiple risks of securing product, obtaining financing, recruiting staff, generating customers and operating a business. The corporate entrepreneur can face an entrenched and stagnant bureaucracy that demands exceptional skills in navigating this corporate maze. Regardless of prior achievements, they still face dismissal in the event of failure or regime change. And if female, there is still the glass ceiling to be penetrated.

Now, let's dig deeper into entrepreneurship and develop an understanding of both these worlds.

THE OWNER ENTREPRENEUR

Over the years I have encountered two overriding concerns of owners, "How do I raise additional financing?" and "How do I generate new customers at a cost I can live with?"

There are basically five sources of entrepreneurial financing.

1) Friends, relatives, neighbors and maxed-out credit cards.

2) Banks, the Small Business Administration (SBA) and for larger companies, venture capital firms.

3) Sale of stock ownership in the company to private investors/lenders.

4) Forming alliances, partnerships, joint ventures and mergers.

5) Funds held in a 401(k), IRA or profit-sharing plan can be rolled over into a new C-corporation's retirement plan. Check out www.benetrends.com for a firm specializing in having these retirement funds released to start or grow a business.

Generally, the first step in obtaining financing is the preparation of a Business Plan (BP). If you are in business to earn money, you are courting disaster if you do not operate under a BP. Your accountant is your best bet to assist you in writing the document.

The Business Plan should be limited to about 20 pages. It should lead with an executive summary of one to three pages and conclude with the projected financial statements. Just ask yourself, "If I was lending the money, what questions would I want answered to feel comfortable that the borrower could pay back the loan and interest on time?" Here are some suggested inquiries.

- What is the background and experience of the borrower?

- Has an attorney been engaged to form the organization and handle legal requirements?

- Has an accountant been hired with experience in preparing BPs and projections?

- Has an office been leased, furnished and staffed?

- What makes the product (or service) better, different and extraordinary?

- How does the product compare to competition?

- Can the product be produced or acquired at a reasonable price?

- What is the potential market and how much has been captured by competitors?

- What is the most effective marketing approach to attract customers—cold calls, direct mail, newspaper ads, radio, TV or the internet?

- Has any ad campaign been test marketed and if so, what are the results to date?

- Have prospective customers been contacted or surveyed?

- Have any employees been hired? For which positions and what is their experience?

- Who will make up the management team and who will sit on the Board of Directors?

- How will the funds be employed?

- Has a one-year "Projection of Operations" been prepared on a monthly basis?

If you can answer these questions with regard to your company, you will have a Business Plan that is receptive to most lenders. Hire your accountant. Together, the two of you can prepare the BP.

The BP should be upbeat and truthful. I have witnessed many a deal fall through because of a misrepresentation. The pervasive feeling was that if we caught one falsehood, how many did we miss?

When making the BP presentation to a lender, be guided by two essentials. First, know the contents flawlessly and then belt it out with conviction. People will be impressed with your passion as much as the very words you speak.

Finally, here is one of the greatest "closes" you will ever encounter. Go eyeball to eyeball with the lender and say, "The reason I included the Projection of Operations on a monthly basis is because it is critical in managing a successful business. First you project, then you compare the actual results with the monthly projections. Next, you account for the differences and then act upon the required changes. In essence, you project, you compare, you account, and you act. This is how I will run the company."

It has worked for me and I'm confident you should experience similar results.

HOW DO I GENERATE NEW CUSTOMERS
AT A COST I CAN LIVE WITH?

Here, we encounter the entrepreneur's eternal quest for more business.

It has been estimated that some 12,000 books have been written on entrepreneurship. In this mix there have a number of outstanding treatises on marketing and selling. Here are highlights of three.

In *Ultimate Small Business Marketing Guide*, author James Stephenson offers 1500 marketing tips and tricks. You are sure to find valuable and relevant ideas and concepts in this exhaustive compendium. *Duct Tape Marketing* by John Jantsch offers a broad spectrum of practical marketing practices and advice. It is well written, concise and most important—it all makes sense for the small business owner. For the next step up from a start-up, there is *Marketing That Works* by Leonard Lodish, professor of marketing at the Wharton School; Howard Morgan, former vice chairman of Idealab; and Shellye Archambeau, CEO of Metricstream. From market-driven strategy to product launch to advertising to PR to branding—it is the whole package.

If you digest these three writings, then virtually any marketing challenge you come up against—you will be well equipped to handle.

THE "CEO STRATEGY FOR

GENERATING NEW CUSTOMERS"

My objective is not to offer you specific marketing solutions. I do not know your product line, customers, competition or market. But what I do know is the "CEO Strategy" that will lead you to the right solution. Just follow these steps.

1. Determine where your product line is better or different from the competition and how it satisfies whatever the customer needs solving.
2. If you don't know, then get out in the field and find out. Take customers to lunch, do research, conduct surveys—do whatever it takes to get answers.
3. Understand that marketing can be synthesized into the three Ms of *Market*Message *Media—and grasp their meaning.
4. As always, the best practice is to hire professionals. This is usually a local ad agency for a start-up or small firm.
5. Call upon advertising agencies and attempt to arrange a "spec" (no cost) presentation based on your potential as a long-term client.
6. If you have not formalized a marketing budget, then estimate 10% of the projected sales for the next six months. Do not be concerned, this number can always be reduced. Just remember, if the budget is too low, the agency will probably walk.
7. Assume the ad agency is excited over your firm's potential and comes back with a proposed marketing campaign. At this point, you are confronted with a

number of critical questions. Does the message seem right for your product and your customers? Does the suggested media make sense in terms of reaching your prospective buyers?

8. If you are satisfied with the response to both questions, the next inquiry should be, "How can we test market the campaign and gather the results before committing the full budget?"

9. At minimum, test the headline and body copy. If feasible, test various media. It is irresponsible to commit the entire budget on an unproven campaign.

10. Most significant, you are to now ask, "If we do commit to the test campaign, what reasonable response can we anticipate?" If the agency balks at answering or offers meaningless generalities, you are probably with the wrong firm.

11. The operational strategy of project, compare, account, and execute also applies to advertising campaigns. If the ad agency cannot project anticipated responses, then what was the mind-set in conceiving the campaign?

12. The marketing objective is to generate a given number of leads or sales for the dollars committed. Even if a particular ad fails, if you can determine why it failed, you are positioned to move forward.

This customer-generating strategy applies to all proposed campaigns from ads in local newspapers to direct mail to internet marketing. You need not know how to write an ad or select media, but you must know the right questions to ask. However, if you follow the 12 step guideline, you can be a winner from the get-go.

THE CORPORATE ENTREPRENEUR

Advances in technology and the growth of globalization have forced the larger firms to constantly innovate in order to remain competitive. In today's world, to stand still is to fall behind.

Thus, the ultimate challenge for modern-day management is to produce consistent profits while creating a workplace environment where corporate entrepreneurs can flourish. Recall the PricewaterhouseCoopers study, where only 29% of innovative ideas originated from employees? This is unacceptable. Management must commit to creating an innovative workplace where corporate entrepreneurs can prosper. Here are four cornerstone requirements.

- New ideas are to be encouraged, processed and rewarded.
- Information Technology (IT) professionals are responsible for collecting, storing, sharing and providing access to corporate data.
- Establish a formal learning center where business skills are promoted.
- A senior officer will oversee and be accountable for the development, funding and execution of the program.

It should also be recognized that corporate entrepreneurs are made, not born. Here are the attributes management should seek to develop.

1. A competitive drive to advance and excel
2. Commitment to lifelong learning
3. Risk-taker—willing to take on unpopular challenges

4. Resiliency—mistakes and failures will occur, but the key is to bounce back
5. Ability to communicate verbally and in writing
6. Accountability when taking on responsibility
7. "People person"—gets along with associates and leads by example
8. Understands the financial consequences of proposals and projects
9. Ethical behavior—co-workers are attracted to trustworthy associates
10. Aware of the opportunities and threats outside the corporate walls

That's quite a list. However, if we are to turn co-workers into corporate entrepreneurs, this is the challenge management must accept. For the most part, these skills can be taught. It should be a CEO's priority to establish a learning center where this transformation can formally take place.

A workforce with trained corporate entrepreneurs will provide an unmatched competitive edge. It will also create an unrivaled source of talent to move up and into the ranks of management. Corporate entrepreneurs truly represent the enterprise's most valuable long-term asset and they need to be cultivated.

THE WRAP-UP

Let's see what we have gained in our discourse on entrepreneurship.

- There are some 35 million enterprises in the USA of self-employed, home-based business operators,

143

independent contractors, professionals, consultants and the like.

- Entrepreneurs come in two sizes—owners and corporate. The owners carry all the risks of operating a business while the corporate folks require special skills to navigate the organizational maze.

- The owner's eternal needs are added financing and generating new customers.

- The five sources of financing range from friends and relatives to banks to the sale of stock to forming alliances to retirement fund

- The Business Plan can be summarized as follows 1) detail borrower's background 2) review legal and accounting 3) list office rented and personnel hired 4) highlight product's attributes 5) compare to competition 6) set forth prior market research and advertising campaigns 7) describe the management team and Board of Directors and 8) provide a one-year operating projection, prepared on a monthly basis.

- In presentations to lenders, always disclose your operating strategy of project, compare, account and execute.

- The "CEO Strategy for Generating New Customers" can make you a winner from the get-go. It can be summarized as follows 1) determine if the product satisfies customer needs compared to the competition 2) do market research 3) grasp the meaning of *Market*Message*Media 4) hire professionals 5) arrange for "spec" presentations 6) project ad budget at

10% of six month's volume 7) evaluate agency's proposed campaign via the three M's 8) test market before committing entire budget 9) at minimum, test headline and body copy 10) project test campaign results 11) institute monthly strategy of project, compare, account and execute and 12) even if a particular ad fails, if you know why it failed, you are positioned to move forward.

- Firms must innovate to remain competitive. In today's world, to stand still is to fall behind.

- The ultimate challenge for modern-day management is to produce consistent profits while creating a workplace environment where corporate entrepreneurs can flourish.

- Management should seek to advance these attributes in cultivating corporate entrepreneurs 1) competitive drive to excel 2) commitment to lifelong learning 3) risk-taking 4) resiliency 5) ability to communicate 6) accountability 7) "people person" 8) understands financials 9) ethical behavior and 10) aware of outside opportunities and threats.

- A workforce of trained corporate entrepreneurs will provide an unmatched competitive advantage.

Entrepreneurship has been the driving force in the growth of American business. Now, it is time to explore foreign opportunities and "going global".

This page intentionally left blank.

CHAPTER 10
GOING GLOBAL

RISE OF THE SMEs

SMEs (small and medium enterprises) have been significant contributors to the growth of international trade. Not just in China and India, but here in the USA where 97% of companies exporting merchandise are SMEs.

Without doubt, the advances in technology—by way of computers, the internet and mobile communications—have opened the door for SMEs to participate in this onslaught. Connectivity has enabled even desktop freelancers to transact worldwide trade at any place and at any time.

To facilitate global trade, SMEs normally operate through export intermediaries and international trade consultants. By contrast, the larger companies may have their own internal global trading department. Generally speaking, SMEs specialize in business to business (B2B) transactions while the larger firms tend to sell directly to consumers.

I believe it would be particularly helpful if we now delve into the basics of international trade.

WHY GO GLOBAL?

Simply consider the fact that for many companies, 95% of their potential customers reside outside the USA. Going global is triggered by the opportunity to,

1) increase sales and profits

2) locate less costly products

3) respond to foreign request for quotations (RFQs)

4) gain economy of scale

5) open new markets to overcome stagnated populations and

6) conduct international internet trading.

Tom Freidman, author of *The World Is Flat*, smartly observed, "You cannot protect yourself to prosperity." He is simply advising that we cannot grow when hiding behind quotas and tariffs. We must get out there and get our share. We must compete in what we know best. Just think "green" and what America can contribute in that movement alone.

Need a wake-up call? Last year, it was reported that a half-million of our tax returns were prepared by accountants in India.

GETTING STARTED

Going global requires the same up-front analysis as seeking to penetrate any major domestic market. On the other hand, transacting overseas business is burdened by regulations, language, culture and risks that border on an unworldly experience.

The first lesson to be learned is this—if your product is not selling here in the USA, forget about exporting. Next, is your product unique and affordable or is it just another commodity? Overseas competitors can normally produce commodity products faster and cheaper. Is management fully committed to going global? Has it provided funding and personnel—and does it understand the extended time frame in penetrating foreign markets?

Normal market research, surveys and direct contact with prospective overseas customers are prohibitively expensive. For SMEs considering exporting, I would suggest a "low-cost probing" approach as follows:

- Visit the trade specialists at the Export Assistance Centers (EACs) of the Department of Commerce. The EACs are located in some 100 cities and offer comprehensive trade, financing and marketing expertise.
- Or visit the local SBA and arrange for a one-on-one session with one of their international professionals. They can provide counseling in trade, marketing, financing and export legal assistance.
- Establish a relationship with a commercial bank that conducts international commerce. They also have specialists that can provide expert consultation and guidance.
- Tap into the literally hundreds of internet sites offering valuable information on going global. Here are four prime sites to launch your search 1) the highly regarded site from Michigan State University, http://www.globaledge.msu.edu 2) the information-packed site of an international trading company http://going-global.com 3) Small Business Administration at http://www.sbaonline.sba.gov and 4) trade compliances and directories at http://www.unzco.com.

The objectives in all visits and searches should be,

1) evaluation of your product's export potential
2) which countries are the best prospects
3) recommendations for foreign representatives and distributors
4) determine what market research is required
5) gather information on licenses, documentation and other exporting requirements
6) analyze shipping options and costs
7) check available government-secured financing
8) inquire as to trade shows, seminars and workshops
9) obtain recommendations for intermediaries such as an export trading company or export management company and
10) suggestions for an international trade consultant.

These intermediaries and consultants can confirm or expand upon the data offered by the EAC, SBA and commercial banks. In addition, they should be a guiding light in preparing an Export Business Plan (EBP)—should the firm seek government-backed financing. The EBP should follow the same basic structure as previously outlined for our domestic Business Plan.

Export trading companies and export management companies are really facilitators. They perform a first-class service in representing their clients in the sale and distribution of their products to international customers. They can also act as the SME's export department.

COMPETITIVE PRICING

The next step is to determine if the product is competitively priced for international markets. This entails accounting for three sets of costs.

1. What is the SME's "product cost" and does this include a profit provision?

2. What added exporting costs may be incurred by way of— product and packaging modifications, shipping charges, insurance, commission to foreign representatives, fees to an export intermediary and the like?

3. What importing costs will be paid by the importer? Is the importer an end user or will the price be further marked up for the retail consumer?

This is where working with an export intermediary or consultant can pay dividends. If the market potential is significant, the SME may be willing to shave the "product cost" to be competitive and penetrate the market.

The very feasibility of launching the export enterprise may depend on this research.

GETTING PAID AND THE LETTER OF CREDIT (L/C)

Let's presume the SME has prudently priced the product. The export management company representing the SME not only agrees, but has found a buyer in China at that price. How does the SME get paid upon shipment?

There are basically four methods of payment in exporting—cash in advance, letter of credit (L/C), sight draft and open credit. Let's see how the process unfolds for the more common L/C transaction.

1. The Chinese buyer will have its bank issue an irrevocable letter of credit (L/C) in favor of the seller SME.

2. The Chinese bank then forwards the L/C to the American bank designated by the SME.

3. The American bank confirms the L/C and agrees to pay the SME once the terms of the L/C have been fulfilled.

4. When the merchandise is loaded on board the ship, a bill of lading is issued and the freight forwarder sends all shipping documents to the SME.

5. The SME then submits all the required documents to the American bank and is paid.

6. The American bank then sends all the documents to the Chinese bank and is reimbursed.

7. When the merchandise arrives in China, the buyer pays off the L/C and the Chinese bank releases the documents. The buyer can now pick up the merchandise.

8. Both banks are appropriately compensated by their respective clients.

There can be numerous variations to this L/C presentation, but in essence, this is how the transaction unfolds. It is to be noted that an export intermediary can handle all the details and the SME's major responsibility is agreeing to the terms of the sale.

MULTINATIONALS

Truth is, multinationals really have no choice but to seek global growth. The driving forces can be summarized as follows:

- Senior management's commitment to its shareholders (and Wall Street) is to produce sustained earnings.

- Achieving these results demands a constant opening up of new markets. With Europe's no-growth population status—and America not far behind—it is vital to attract new customer bases worldwide.

- Top-line growth resulting from global sales renders these multinationals even more competitive and earnings-friendly.

- A growing middle class of foreign customers creates an open invitation for expansion-minded multinationals.

Forward-thinking foreign countries may also encourage such trade. If successful, the multinationals may be enticed to build on-site facilities to satisfy local demand as well as export back to the mother country.

GLOBAL LEADERSHIP

I firmly believe one of the greatest opportunities for an enterprising corporate entrepreneur lies in the management of global growth. Consider the following four books on global leadership.

Working Global Smart by Ernest Gundling. The author sets forth 12 people skills that are essential to global success. They range from establishing credibility to evaluating people to strategic planning to managing change. While simple enough, they take on added dimensions when related to foreign language, culture and business style. Therefore, these skills should be initially developed in domestic operations before committing to a global enterprise.

The Mind of the CEO by Jeffrey Garten. After some 40 interviews with CEOs worldwide, the author concludes that they are not as powerful and astute as we have been led to believe. They face daunting challenges, ranging from coordinating short and long-term objectives to projecting global goals that cannot realistically be achieved. The book reads well and is meaningful. However, I do not share Garten's vision of multinational's greater participation in resolving society's social and political needs. Management may possess worldly knowledge but their perspective is too skewed by their corporate obligation to stakeholders.

Leadership Without Borders by Ed Cohen. The author conducted over 50 interviews with global leaders who have worked and resided in more than 60 countries. He concludes that managing in the global frontier demands a new kind of leadership. Just consider the challenge of managing French engineers who are employed by a Swedish company but work full time at a hydro-electric plant in China. He calls for new global competencies to manage interconnected cultures, languages, social settings and complex business transactions. It appears that one has to think as a "global citizen" before one can become an accomplished global manager.

Global Literacies by Robert Rosen, Patricia Digh, Marshall Singer and Carl Phillips. The authors recognize that co-workers are not only a firm's most valuable asset but also its major competitive advantage. Thus, progressive organizations need to marshal their people to become globally literate and blend corporate culture with world cultures. The key is to appreciate that while all countries face common concerns, each responds differently in accordance with its embedded culture. Once this uniqueness is understood, global strategy can be instituted.

GLOBAL GUIDELINES

Now that we can appreciate the extraordinary opportunity for American enterprises to participate in international trade, consider the following global guidelines.

Guideline # 1: Just as we should not export products that do not sell well in the USA, neither should we attempt to manage international transactions before the leadership skills are developed domestically.

Guideline # 2: You must make the all-out commitment to become a global citizen and understand that local culture is paramount. For example, German folks appreciate starting and stopping a meeting on time. Latin Americans are offended by pushing strict compliance to a specific time.

Guideline # 3: Never forget that co-workers must be indoctrinated to recognize the growth potential in global trade and that foreign folks are unique and must be engaged accordingly. With this mind-set, the enterprise is poised to enter the era of globalization.

Guideline # 4: As with Einstein's relativity theories, relationships do matter. The same holds true with globalization. In international trade, cultivating relationships at all levels is a precursor to a successful venture.

In other words, hone your skills at home before going global, appreciate local culture and become globally literate, indoctrinate globalization into the corporate culture and learn to cultivate international relationships at all levels.

THE WRAP-UP

The prospect of going global today is truly a historic opportunity. Let's see how much of the gateway we have opened up.

- SMEs have been significant contributors to the growth of international trade. In the USA, they account for 97% of the companies exporting.

- For many companies, 95% of their prospects reside outside the country.

- Going global is triggered by the opportunity to 1) increase sales and profits 2) locate less-costly products 3) respond to foreign requests for quotations 4) gain economy of scale 5) open new markets to overcome stagnated populations and 6) conduct international internet trading.

157

- America must compete in what it knows best. Just think "green" and what we can contribute in that movement alone.

- Going global requires the same up-front analysis as when seeking to penetrate any major domestic market. The risks lie in dealing with foreign regulations, language and culture.

- Lesson # 1: if your product is not selling in the USA, forget about exporting.

- Lesson # 2: if your product is a commodity, avoid competitive countries.

- Lesson # 3: do not consider exporting unless management is fully committed. This means committing funding, personnel and understanding the extended time frame in penetrating foreign markets.

- Begin the export venture with the low-cost probing of specialists at Export Assistance Centers, the SBA and commercial banks. Launch an internet search on the four recommended sites.

- The objectives of such visits and searches are to 1) evaluate your product's export potential 2) determine which counties are better prospects 3) get the names of recommended representatives and distributors 4) discover how much market research is required 5) gather information on exporting requirements 6) analyze shipping options and costs 7) attain counseling on government-secured financing 8) inquire as to trade shows, seminars and workshops and 9) obtain recommendations for intermediaries.

- Export trading companies and export management companies can facilitate the sale and distribution to international customers. Many can also act as the SME's export department.

- Export intermediaries and/or consultants should participate in determining product pricing for foreign markets.

- There are four payment options in international trade— cash in advance, letter of credit (L/C), sight draft and open credit. The L/C is the most common transaction.

- The L/C transaction unfolds as follows 1) the foreign buyer has its bank issue an irrevocable L/C in favor of the USA seller 2) the L/C is sent to the seller's USA bank which issues a confirming letter 3) after the merchandise has been shipped, the seller presents all required documents to its bank and is paid 4) the USA bank then sends the documents to the foreign bank and is reimbursed 5) when the merchandise arrives, the foreign buyer pays off the L/C and receives the documents to pick up the merchandise and 6) bank fees are paid by their respective clients.

- There can be many variations to a L/C transaction. The export intermediary normally can handle all of the details. The seller's major responsibility is agreeing to the terms of the sale.

- Many larger organizations require global growth in order to produce sustained earnings. To overcome stagnating populations, it is vital that companies open new markets worldwide. This top-line growth renders multinationals even more competitive and earnings-friendly.

- Corporate entrepreneurs have an extraordinary opportunity in the management of global growth.

- The four essential guidelines for corporate entrepreneurs seeking to engage in international trade are 1) develop leadership skills domestically before taking on international management 2) become a global citizen and appreciate that local culture is paramount 3) recognize the growth potential in global trade and that foreign folks are unique and must be approached according and 4) cultivate relationships at all levels, for it is a precursor to global success.

If you follow these global fundamentals you will be primed to enter the rewarding world of international trade. Now, let's consider the golden rules of business ethics.

CHAPTER 11
BUSINESS ETHICS

DOING THINGS "RIGHT"

Business ethics is all about doing things "right."

The question then becomes, what is "right"? Is it "right," according to religious or moral codes, legal statutes, local customs, regulatory agency's rules, corporate codes or market forces? And to which country or religion or corporation does this refer?

Most of us believe we know the difference between right and wrong. True enough, but how many know about ethical dilemmas, where both sides can be considered "right"?

Few business issues are as conflicting and challenging as business ethics. For example, let's take an ethical view of an organization. There are those who believe that the sole purpose of a company listed on the New York Stock Exchange is to maximize profits for its stockholders.

A second group holds that companies have an obligation beyond their stockholders. They believe organizations have a commitment to stakeholders such as employees, customers, suppliers and the local community. Then there are social theorists who put forth the concept that enterprises must assume certain society responsibilities.

Let's bypass the theoretical and philosophical considerations and come up with a practical program for business ethics that will satisfy a practicing CEO. The first step is to acquire an understanding of the major complexities involved in business ethics and then seek out solutions.

WHY THE SURGE IN ETHICAL MISBEHAVIOR?

There are a multitude of reasons for the recent onslaught of misdeeds. Here are some of the more significant issues:

1. The growth, complexity and globalization of businesses have resulted in an ever widening gulf between management and shareholders.

2. Management tends to become entrenched and self-perpetuating in the absence of a take-over bid or a major collapse in earnings.

3. The huge amount of money to be made in senior corporate positions becomes an overwhelming temptation for non-ethical behavior, especially where oversight is overlooked.

4. An "entitlement" mind-set has developed that justifies excessive salaries, obscene stock options and offensive golden parachutes.

5. There is a deceptive attitude that "as long as it's legal, it must be ethical."

6. The need to meet or beat Wall Street's quarterly projections—drives questionable business practices that are detrimental to sustained growth and long-term success.

7. GAAP regulations are not always ethically friendly. They are so flexible that management has many options to manipulate valuations as well as bottom-line results.

8. Complex financial instruments such as derivatives—with the overvaluation of underlying securities—can be both unethical and illegal.

9. Management may rationalize unethical actions in foreign countries by saying, "It's the local custom and legal over there."

10. There is the ethical predicament of "If we did not do it, the company would have to lay people off or even shut down the plant."

ETHICS IN THE WORKPLACE

Human Resources: In some enterprises, this is the area of greatest legal concern. Liability can arise from discrimination on the basis of gender, age, religion, race or sexual orientation. Legal responsibility also can flow from sexual harassment. You can now add to the list smoking, weight preference, attractiveness, drug testing and unauthorized computer use for personal gain. Whether the misbehavior also originates in hiring, compensation or advancement, you can certainly appreciate the need for ethical guidance.

Production: It would appear that a company's ethical responsibility is to produce a product that performs as advertised. However, what if the product also causes pollution? What if prolonged usage can cause serious illness? What if production outside the USA has quality-control problems?

Finances and Accounting: The opportunity for unethical behavior is ever present. Think about "creative accounting" that stretches GAAP to the limit and results in misleading statements. Consider the morality of exorbitant executive compensation, excessive stock options and extravagant golden parachutes—when not tied to performance.

Marketing and Sales: While puffery is acceptable, deceptive "bait and switch" tactics are not. However, marketers do employ schemes such as "introductory price offers" that soon escalate and become overwhelmingly burdensome. This can range from credit card rate changes to the crisis caused by adjustable-rate mortgages. The opportunity for questionable marketing practices abounds from promoting tasty but unhealthy products to children to exaggerated advertising claims that are legally cured via small-print footnotes.

Even with this brief trip-around in the workplace, we can all agree on the need for ethical guidance. There is one other area to explore before we seek solutions.

ETHICAL DILEMMAS

Ethical dilemmas come into play when basic values are in conflict and there is justification for taking either side of the controversy. Here are two illustrations:

Dilemma #1: The Law vs. the Town

There is a mid-sized plant in a small New England town that has been losing money for the past three years. Not only are the employees facing layoffs but most of the townspeople are financially dependent on the plant staying open. In desperation, the owner travels to southeastern Asia and gets a commitment for a major order. There is only one problem.

As is the country's custom, a 5% under-the-table cash payment is required. This "bribe," which is customary in that country, nevertheless violates USA regulations. So, do you pay the money and keep your company and the townspeople flourishing for the next five years or do you turn it down and prepare to close shop and destroy the lives of so many good folks?

Do you mitigate matters by considering the payment a commission expense? Or, how about telling yourself, "When in Rome, do as the Romans do"?

Dilemma #2: The Company vs. Best Friend

You have recently been promoted to a senior management position and now participate in all strategy sessions. At today's meeting, you learned that the division, headed by your closest friend and next-door neighbor, is scheduled to be shut down and everyone dismissed. All participants were cautioned to keep this decision absolutely secret to avoid any preliminary upheaval prior to the announcement.

Your dilemma is that you know that your neighbor is about to make a substantial down payment on a larger home. To make matters worse, he is meeting this weekend with the admissions committee of an exclusive country club.

Do you endanger your position with the company that you worked years to achieve or do you let your best friend drown in financial debt?

Is there a right or wrong answer? Or does it come down to one's conscience and risk assessment?

There are a number of suggested approaches to resolving ethical dilemmas. They basically revolve around asking ethical questions and assigning a sliding-scale value to each response. The final question asks if your answers would remain the same—if you knew these responses would be exposed to family, friends and company management.

THE ETHICS AGENDA

The goal of a business ethics program is simple enough—get all employees to behave in a preferred manner. Here, in summary fashion is a four-step ethics agenda.

Step 1: Have top management make an all-out commitment to install and carry out a business ethics program. Assign a senior level executive to take charge and assume responsibility for the program's success. All managers must demonstrate their support and act accordingly.

Step 2: Publish a Code of Ethics which highlights the firm's values along the lines suggested by the Josephson Institute of Ethics—trustworthiness and honesty, respect and tolerance, accountability and responsibility, caring and sharing, justice and equality and community service.

Step 3: Issue a Code of Conduct setting forth workplace behavior covering dress code, coming to work on time, no drugs, avoiding discrimination, prohibiting harassment of any kind, non-acceptance of gifts and similar unacceptable activities.

Step 4: Communicate and promote the codes repeatedly and post them in relevant locations.

It should be noted that many firms prefer combining the Code of Ethics and the Code of Conduct into one document. To view an excellent code featuring ethics and conduct, go to http://info.ethicspoint.com/about/ethicspolicy/ and review "Our Ethics Policy." The EthicsPoint company specializes in the field.

Larger firms may have a compliance officer to administer the codes and hear complaints. All codes must be reviewed by legal counsel to ensure compliance with local, state and federal laws.

We should recognize that managing business ethics is a process that requires constant nurturing. The codes will soon become meaningless unless the CEO and top brass support the ethics program and it becomes part of the corporate culture.

When ethical misdeeds surfaced at GE, Jack Welch immediately fired the transgressors. Further, he let it be known that future violators would automatically be discharged. There would be no second chances.

BOTTOM-LINE BENEFITS

What are the benefits of installing a business ethics program? In summary, they can be highlighted as follows.

Legal: Look to prevent discriminatory behavior, sexual harassment and the like—thus avoiding the high cost of litigation and liability. The Federal Sentencing Guidelines permit the reduction of fines if the guilty company has an ongoing program to encourage ethical behavior.

Operations: A company that develops an ethical culture can inspire trust and fellowship leading to productivity gains. This can also spill over to the relationships with customers and suppliers.

Profitability: A company that builds an ethical reputation and offers products that perform as advertised— has a distinct competitive edge in the marketplace.

Regardless of what the naysayers say, there is no substitute for doing the right thing. It is a feel-good feeling that motivates most people.

THE WRAP-UP

Let's recap the critical components and complexities of business ethics.

- Business ethics are all about doing things "right." The question then becomes, "What is right?"

- Is "right" determined by religious codes, legal statutes, regulatory agencies or market forces? And to which country laws or religion does this refer to?

- The surge in ethical misbehavior can be attributed to 1) the complexity and globalization of businesses resulting in widening the gap between management and stockholders 2) management becoming entrenched and self-perpetuating 3) excessive compensation 4) an "entitlement" mind-set 5) the attitude that "as long as it is legal, it must be ethical" 6) the need to beat Wall Street's quarterly numbers 7) manipulating GAAP regulations 8) overvaluation of the underlying securities of complex financial instruments such as "derivatives" 9) management rationalizing that "it's the local custom over there" and 10) management's fall-back position of "If we did not do it, the company would have to lay people off and even shut down the plant."

- The major areas of concern for unethical behavior in the workplace originate from discrimination and harassment, product liability, misleading financial statements and questionable advertising claims.

- There are no right or wrong answers in ethical dilemmas. It may all come down to one's conscience, risk assessment and whether the party can handle the exposure to family, friends and company management.

- The four-step agenda for establishing a business ethics program include 1) having management make an all-out commitment to install and implement the program 2) publishing a Code of Ethics 3) issuing a Code of

Conduct and 4) communicating and promoting the codes repeatedly.

- Managing the ethics program is a process that requires constant nurturing. The CEO and top brass must support the effort until ethics become ingrained into the corporate culture.

- The bottom-line benefits of instituting an ethics program can be seen in 1) reducing legal liability 2) inspiring a trust that promotes fellowship and productivity and 3) building a reputation that produces a competitive edge.

We have now arrived at our concluding chapter—which I intriguingly call Transformation.

This page intentionally left blank.

CHAPTER 12
TRANSFORMATION

AS FAR AS YOU WANT TO GO

You now have the skills to manage most any business challenge that comes your way in this constantly changing environment.

I know this, because you have acquired an awareness and understanding that ranges from strategy to innovation, customers to marketing, cash flow to profitability, employees to management, entrepreneurship to globalization and product lines to business ethics. You now have insight into the whole package.

You can go as far as you want to go. Let me prove it by highlighting what you already know.

YOU KNOW THE INS AND OUTS OF STRATEGY

You know that strategy is all about having a realistic plan to attain specific objectives. That great strategy requires a bold vision. Lou Gerstner had such a vision when he converted IBM from a hardware company with low profit margins to a software and solutions firm with exceptional returns.

You are aware that strategic positioning is really about focusing on being distinctive and different. Just strategizing to doing things better is an open invitation for competitive penetration.

From vision to going global, you have mastered the 10-point strategic plan for companies small and large.

On a personal level, you have adopted the mind-set of viewing operational issues in terms of "Was it better or different—or neither?"

YOU KNOW WHY THE CUSTOMER RULES

You know the customer rules because the customer is the source of cash flow, profitability and everyone's next paycheck. You want all the customers you can get, but they must be profitable.

If a skill is relevant to a customer, you know that, "the company must develop it, or hire it, or acquire it, or license it or find a business partner who will provide it." Customers are more attracted to products that provide solutions than bells and whistles.

You now know that loyal customers are one of the company's prime assets. That it costs five to eight times more to gain a new customer than to retain an existing one. You are aware that a happy customer will recommend to three others while an unhappy one will spread negativity to nine.

You recognize that lunching with top customers is a low-cost initiative that can produce high-value research.

YOU KNOW ALL ABOUT MARKETING

You know that market research can lead to fact-based marketing that can be quantified, tracked, measured and evaluated for ROI (return on investment).

You have identified the three M's of *Market*Message*Media as the who, what and where of marketing. Who is the target market? What message will motivate them? Where can you reach them in media? You now approach test marketing in terms of low-cost strategies such as e-mail, pay-per-click, direct mail or even local cable TV.

You appreciate that traditional advertising is generally so wide and broad that it is ineffective except for the larger firms. You are intrigued by direct response marketing which is primarily focused on generating qualified responses. Campaigns such as direct mail and e-mail are totally dependent on the content of the message and the quality of the lists.

You recognize that social networking sites such as Google, Facebook, LinkedIn and Twitter have experienced gargantuan growth and represent a tipping point in internet marketing.

YOU KNOW THE SECRETS OF FINANCIALS

You know you cannot run a successful business without knowing what you own or owe out or if you have enough cash to meet next week's payroll.

You understand that the Balance Sheet presents the financial position of the company as of a given date. That the Income Statement (Profit and Loss) matches income and expenses over a given period such as, "For the Year Ending December 31, 20XX." You appreciate that Footnotes to financial statements are highly significant and should be critically reviewed.

You are aware that there are gaps in GAAP because the rules are flexible and subject to various interpretations. Thus, financial statements reflect management's assumptions, estimates, judgments and adjustments to the raw financial data.

You are cognizant of the fact that it is the integrity of management and the certification of the CPA firm that assure the validity of the financial statements.

YOU KNOW THE ART OF MANAGEMENT

You fully grasp the great operating strategy of monthly projecting, comparing, accounting for variances and executing required changes. That this strategy represents the highest form of managerial accountability. This strategy holds true whether dealing with a start-up, SME, subsidiary or the mother company.

You are mindful that many companies that were highly promoted in best-selling books subsequently crashed because they failed to respond to a changing environment. Further, you recognize that awareness and adaptability are the hallmarks of an astute and accomplished CEO.

You understand that a competitive drive, along with lifelong learning, risk-taking and resiliency—all point to leadership as a maturing process. This lends further credence to leaders being made and not born.

You have adopted the 30 benchmarks of the "CEO Imperative" that will serve as your personal operating guideline and checklist. You have come to appreciate that never before have corporate leaders needed to know so much about so many issues on so large a scale that will change so often.

YOU KNOW ALL ABOUT INNOVATION

You know that 46% of innovative ideas come from customers, suppliers and the marketplace— with only 29% originating from employees. You realize that management must encourage greater co-worker participation.

You are aware that the four phases of the innovation process revolve around 1) establishing a database of submitted ideas 2) evaluating and selecting the best 3) producing the product and 4) testing and launching.

You are familiar with the fact that highly creative ideas usually come from employees dealing directly with customers. For example, 800 suggestions flowed from an innovative receptionist who asked customers calling to complain, "What would you do about it?"

You are mindful that some adventurous marketers are now looking to customers as co-creators of innovation on social networking sites. The rewards can be extraordinary but the risk of a highly publicized rejection can be devastating.

YOU KNOW PRODUCT LINE STRATEGY

You know that in product line strategy, a firm cannot be all things to all people and still remain profitable. The objective is to gain a competitive edge via product leadership (think

Microsoft) or operational excellence (think Wal-Mart) or customer intimacy (think British Airways).

You have totally absorbed the 15 steps in upgrading an existing product line. These same procedures also apply to launching a new line.

You are now aware that commoditization can be overcome through customization, branding, design, opening new markets, new product offerings and introducing new services.

You recognize that disruptive technology can overtake even the best-managed companies. The key is early awareness of the competition and adapting to the required changes.

YOU KNOW ALL ABOUT
KNOWLEDGE EMPLOYEES (KEs)

You now know what employees want and what management expects in return.

You know that knowledge employees (KEs) are co-workers who use information in carrying out their assignments. The recruitment, training, empowerment and motivation of KEs are the trademarks of an elite management.

You are aware that Peter Drucker has cautioned, "Partnership with the responsible worker is the only way to improve productivity."

You have learned that every employee can become a business person. You have been informed that housekeepers, bellhops and doormen at the Ritz-Carlton Hotel in San Francisco have been authorized to spend $2,000 to satisfy a customer's complaint. You recognize there are creative approaches to upgrading the employee/management relationship—ranging from open-book-management to participation in strategic planning to structuring service departments as business units.

After becoming familiar with the Saatchi case, you now realize that a company's human capital truly can be its most valuable asset.

YOU KNOW THE ENTREPRENEURSHIP STORY

You now know that there is a global awakening for self-expression and that entrepreneurship is brought on by advances in computers, the internet and mobile communications. Entrepreneurs come in two sizes—owners and corporate.

You have become familiar with the owner's eternal need for financing and gaining new customers. You are aware of the five sources of financing ranging from friends and relatives to banks to sale of stock to forming alliances to utilizing retirement funds. You know that employing the "CEO Strategy For Generating New Customers" can make you a winner from the get-go.

You recognize that the ultimate challenge for management is to produce sustained profits while creating a workplace environment where corporate entrepreneurs can flourish.

You now concur that management should seek to cultivate the following entrepreneurial attributes— commitment to lifelong learning, risk-taking, resiliency, ability to communicate, accountability, comprehending financials, getting along with co-workers, ethical behavior and awareness of opportunities and threats outside the company.

YOU KNOW WHY AND HOW TO GO GLOBAL

You know that 97% of U.S. exporters are SMEs and for many companies 95% of their prospects reside outside the country. You recognize "going global" offers the opportunity to open new markets, increase profits, locate less-costly products and respond to foreign requests for quotations.

You understand that a newcomer to exporting should begin the process with the low-cost probing of specialists at the Export Assistance Centers, the Small Business Administration and local commercial banks—and visiting the suggested sites on the internet. You now know the 10 essential questions that must be raised with the export specialists.

After reviewing the Letter of Credit transaction, you now have a basic familiarity as to how the export payment process unfolds.

You are aware that corporate entrepreneurs have an extraordinary opportunity in managing their company's global growth. They need to1) hone their skills at home before going global 2) become a "global citizen" 3) indoctrinate globalization into the corporate culture and 4) cultivate international relationships at all levels.

YOU KNOW THE FUNDAMENTALS
OF BUSINESS ETHICS

You know that the surge in ethical misbehavior can be attributed to 1) the widening gap between management and shareholders 2) entrenchment of management 3) excessive compensation 4) an entitlement mind-set 5) the attitude that "as long as it is legal, it must be ethical" 6) beating Wall Street's quarterly numbers 7) manipulating GAAP guidelines 8) unregulated complex financial instruments 9) foreign customs that differ from U.S. regulations and 10) the fallback position of "If we did not do it, we would have had to lay off people and shut down the plant."

You recognize that the major areas of legal concern stem from discrimination and harassment, product liability, misleading financial statements and questionable advertising claims.

You are aware that the four-phase agenda for establishing an ethics program includes— management's all-out commitment, publishing a Code of Ethics, issuing a Code of Conduct and promoting the codes repeatedly.

You know that management must fully support the effort until ethics become ingrained into the corporate culture.

****

I believe we can both agree that a certain transformation has taken place. You now have acquired the overall know-how and insight to grow and manage a profitable enterprise.

I would strongly suggest that you revisit the 10 point strategic plan for companies large and small and constantly review the 30 components of the "CEO Imperative." These are classic guidelines and checklists of a CEO's game plan.

Keep in mind that much of your success will depend upon your ability to communicate and interact with employees and customers. Therefore, let me close with a rather profound observation by Zig Ziglar, "You don't have to be great to start, but you have to start to be great."

This page intentionally left blank.

SOME PARTING THOUGHTS

Before parting company, I would like to offer some thoughts on implementing the knowledge you have acquired.

FOR THE CORPORATE ENTREPRENEUR

Do you have any special expertise covering increasing sales, reducing costs, improving product quality, upgrading employee productivity, getting new customers, providing innovative ideas, increasing profitability—or any other capability that would enhance the company's performance?

If the answer is yes to any of the above, then you must speak up at the next company meeting. You must offer solutions in any area where you have this special knowledge. Do not fear public speaking. There are only two requirements to be an effective speaker—know what you are talking about and belt it out like you really mean it. People will buy into your passion.

What if you do not have any exceptional expertise?

Then employ "the art of the leading question." This is powerful stuff. No matter what the subject, you can now contribute smartly by asking a penetrating question. For example, if the meeting is about advertising—ask if the company plans to test market. If the discussion centers on obtaining financing—ask about the contents of the Business Plan. If the topic turns to the company's product line—ask if they have considered upgrading the line employing the 15 step guideline.

You are now capable of enriching any meeting on virtually any phase of the operation. Try to obtain an advance copy of the meeting's agenda so you can come prepared with guidelines, checklists—and questions.

If you have come up with an extraordinary solution that could significantly benefit the organization, request the opportunity to conduct your own seminar or workshop. If this is not feasible, consider writing a memorandum covering the problem, your solution and the financial benefits to the company.

FOR THE OWNER ENTREPRENEUR

If you are out there on your own, your two major concerns are probably cash flow and getting customers at a cost you can live with.

As for financing, review the five sources of funding and how to prepare a Business Plan that banks will find compelling. Then act.

If your company markets locally, just follow the "CEO Strategy for Getting New Customers." Consider direct response marketing. It is relatively inexpensive and focuses solely on lead generation and sales. For a quick online education, visit www.dankennedy.com. Then hire a local professional and get started.

Entrepreneurs are a self-motivated group. If things work out, they are always on the hunt for more. If things fail, they find out why—and they have the resiliency to move on and up.

I should know, I have been building companies throughout most of my business life—and it has been fun.

My friend, you have the business know-how to put all this vast knowledge to work. It is time for you to get started and bring to life your most cherished dreams. Always remember the wisdom of the Roman philosopher Seneca, "Luck is what happens when preparation meets opportunity."

Good luck and thank you for letting me be a part of your success.

This page intentionally left blank.

INDEX

For your convenience, the Index is classified into three sections: **BUSINESS LUMINARIES**, followed by **COMPANIES** and concluding with **BUSINESS STRATEGIES AND TACTICS**.

BUSINESS LUMINARIES

Jagdish Sheth, Book, THE SELF DESTRUCTIVE HABITS OF GOOD COMPANIES: P. 83

Michael J. Silverstein & John Butman, Book, TREASURE HUNT: INSIDE THE MIND OF THE NEW CUSTOMER: P. 42

Adrian Slywotzky & David Morrison, Book, THE PROFIT ZONE: P. 19

Walter J. Smith et al, Book, COMING TO CONCURRENCE: P. 41

James Stephenson, Book, ULTIMATE SMALL BUSINESS GUIDE: P. 139

Potter Stewart, Quotation by the Justice of the Supreme Court: P. 34

Thomas Stewart, Book, INTELLECTUAL CAPITAL: P. 129

Paul Stoltz, Book, ADVERSITY QUOTIENT: P. 86

Robert Tomasko, Book, BIGGER ISN'T ALWAYS BETTER: P. 87

Joe Tucci, Article, THE ROLE OF THE CEO IN INNOVATION: P. 94

David Verklin & Bernice Kanner, Book, WATCH THIS, LISTEN UP, CLICK HERE: P. 51

Stephen & Shannon Wall, Book, THE NEW STRATEGISTS: P. 125-126

Jeff Weiner, CEO, LinkedIn: P. 47

Jack Welch, Book, STRAIGHT FROM THE GUT: P. 6, 88

Professor Monica Worline, Employee – Management Study: P. 128-129

Jerry Yang, Yahoo founder's commentary on REAL TIME: PREPARING FOR THE AGE OF THE NEVER SATISFIED CUSTOMER: P.20

Zig Ziglar, Quotation: P. 183

Mark Zuckerberg, founder, Facebook: P. X, 47

COMPANIES

BUSINESS STRATEGIES AND TACTICS

Management

Marketing

Transformation

This page intentionally left blank.

National Praise

"I only wish I had BE SMARTER THAN A CEO IN 30 DAYS to utilize in the Management Training Programs I was responsible for in my capacity as IBM Director Of Management Development. It is a must read for people on the fast track."
Walter Schiff, retired IBM Executive
and Consultant to Technology Companies - Florida

"A stimulating and beneficial collection of sage advice! Whether you are a seasoned veteran who wants a shot of inspiration, or a newbie with a dream, this book is a must read. It will definitely be a "go to guide" on my bookshelf. Thanks J.J. Medney, for succinctly sharing this wealth of knowledge."
Christine Bennett, Senior Account Manager
SCA Promotions, Inc. - Dallas, Texas

"During my years in business, I have read many self help and business books. BE SMARTER THAN A CEO IN 30 DAYS has more usable knowledge on one page than most books do in a chapter. I plan on giving copies to all my associates and recommend it to any business person who wants to improve the way his/her business is run."
Dr. Bruce Foote, COO
Family Dental Group - Flint, Michigan

"Who needs an MBA? BE SMARTER THAN A CEO IN 30 DAYS gets to the heart of smart business thinking. Whether you are climbing the corporate ladder, or going down an entrepreneurial road, J.J. Medney provides a roadmap for success."
Chris Ponzio, SVP
Levlane Advertising/Public Relations/Interactive
Philadelphia, Pennsylvania

"A book you will keep returning to for inspiration on running a successful business."
Paul Telenson, Senior Vice President
BeamPines Inc. - New York, New York